DON'T TRY THIS AT HOME

DON'T TRY THIS AT HOME DON'T TRY THIS AT HOME DON'T TRY THIS AT HOME DON'T

DON'T TRY THIS AT HOME

How to Win a Sumo Match,

Catch a Great White Shark,

Start an Independent Nation, and

Other Extraordinary Feats

(for Ordinary People)

Hunter S. Fulghum

BROADWAY BOOKS

NEW YORK

BROADWAY

Broadway Books titles may be purchased for business or
promotional use or for special sales. For information,
please write to: Special Markets Department,
Random House, Inc., 1540 Broadway, New York, NY 10036.

PRINTED IN THE UNITED STATES OF AMERICA

BROADWAY BOOKS and its logo, a letter B bisected on the
diagonal, are trademarks of Broadway Books,
a division of Random House, Inc.

Visit our Web site at www.broadwaybooks.com

First edition published 2002.

Library of Congress Cataloging-in-Publication Data

Fulghum, Hunter S. (Hunter Samuel)
Don't try this at home : how to win a *sumo* match,
catch a great white shark, and start an independent nation,
and other extraordinary feats (for ordinary people) /
Hunter S. Fulghum.— 1st ed.
p. cm.
ISBN 0-7679-1159-8
1. Adventure and adventurers. 2. Daredevils. 3. Escapes.
4. Rescues. 5. Survival skills. I. Title.

G525 .F957 2002
904—dc21
2002018407

5 7 9 10 8 6 4

DESIGNED BY JENNIFER ANN DADDIO
ILLUSTRATED BY TY AND SALLY POLLARD

Here's to you.

You know who you are.

CONTENTS

CONTENTS

SPECIAL THANKS

In researching this book, I found myself having conversations in which I asked questions such as "I know this would never happen, but if it did, how would I do it?" Often, I followed that with "No, really, I am *serious.*"

The most common response was silence, which suggested someone was rolling his eyes in disbelief—or initiating a phone trace.

Not that I was surprised. Some of the things I wanted to know were, admittedly, out there and then some. Asking the U.S. Mint, for example, about how they protect the nation's gold reserves at the depository at Fort Knox, and exactly how one would go about removing that gold (without their blessing), I was met with some skepticism. Likewise, the Bureau of Reclamation and the fine people at Hoover Dam had some reservations about addressing the matter of swimming through the bypass tunnels at the dam.

To give them credit, they quite happily supplied me with endless facts and figures. How much concrete was poured at Hoover?—4,360,000 cubic yards. What is there to see in the Fort Knox area?—the Patton Museum. How exciting.

What I really wanted to know was what I would characterize as the good stuff: like the details of the construction of the gold vaults at the fort and the access codes of the security system; detailed plans of the spillways at Hoover Dam; a schematic diagram of the security system of the Louvre gallery where the *Mona Lisa* is kept and, if it's not too much trouble, the guard-rotation schedule.

To these sorts of questions, when I was even bold enough to ask, the response was silence, and a funny clicking noise on the phone as the trace began. Understandable, but frustrating from my point of view.

So you will understand just how gratifying it was when a few souls suspended their better judgment for a few minutes and listened to me without concluding that I was utterly crazy or dangerous. Because of people like them, I can actually tell you how much dynamite it takes to put out an oil-well fire, or what is the right dose of what tranquilizer to administer to a 500-pound alligator.

It is to these people that I must offer grateful thanks, for the information, the ideas, and, most of all, their willingness to suspend their disbelief and answer the questions:

- Karla Anderson
- Lt. Mark Anderson
- Deputy Vail Bello, Sonoma County Sheriff's Department
- Lt. Brauna Carl and Captain "X," U.S. Navy
- Channel Swimming Association
- Roman Dial
- Evergreen Veterinary Hospital

SPECIAL THANKS

- Larry Flak, Boots 'n Coots
- Scott Gustafson, DemTech
- Stacy Loizeaux, Controlled Demolition, Inc.
- Neal at the FBI—thanks for trying
- Dr. Skip Nelson
- "Art" and "Leo," Resident Area 51/Alien Experts
- Mike "short-arms" Raftery, Turner Construction Company
- Vern Tejas
- U.S. Department of Energy
- Anatoly Zak, Russianspaceweb.com

I would also be seriously remiss in my manners if I neglected to extend my gratitude to the people who did the deal, handled the contracts, and periodically propped up my ego: Jim Becker, Andy Mayer, and the becker&mayer! Wrecking Crew; and Charlie Conrad and the very fine (and patient) people at Broadway Books. Thanks as well to Ty and Sally Pollard for the wonderful illustrations.

And finally, a special thanks to Marcie DiPietro and Rebecca Cole, who read, edited, coaxed, suggested, and occasionally threatened. It's a better book for your efforts.

Thank you all very, very much.

INTRODUCTION, HAND-WAVING, AND DENIALS

Before we begin, the author would like to publicly state that no lawyers were *seriously* injured in the production of this book.

Along the walls of the bookstores are shelves stuffed with "how to" books: how to scuba dive, fly, snowboard, climb, rappel, river raft, parachute, hang glide, etc. Around the corner are the shops that sell scuba tanks, climbing paraphernalia and ropes, snow gear, backpacks, tents, and other trappings and essentials for the activities we have discovered a taste (if not a talent) for.

Interestingly, as time has passed, our interests in physical activities move closer to the border of suicidal. Why? Perhaps it is the proliferation of NO FEAR T-shirts and overpriced cross-trainers. It's hard to say.

Whatever the reasons, and given the fairly dangerous things we are willing to try, it is interesting to consider where this might lead. If the average man or woman will leap off a bridge tied to a bungee cord, what else might he or she consider trying—assuming the proper instruction was provided?

That question was the genesis of this book. Over time it grew to a list of experiences, experiences out on the edge (and beyond in some cases) that a person might try if only he knew how. In turn, this led to an examination of how to accomplish them (and those odd questions to people who knew). The results of that process are presented here.

For purposes of clarity, each scenario in this book is presented with four essential groups of information. The first element of each activity is WHAT YOU WILL NEED, a list of the essential material and equipment you will need to have on hand to proceed. The list is by no means inflexible and may require some modification or amendment, depending on the situation and personal preferences.

The second element is TIME REQUIRED. These are estimates based on past experience and expert opinion, and it is a given that some variation in timing is to be expected, either due to circumstances or personal style and physical abilities. Except where times are stated as specific requirements, treat TIME REQUIRED as a general guideline only.

The third section is the BACKGROUND portion, devoted to providing some history and perspective, with the occasional word of wisdom from the experts in the field. While the background is not absolutely essential to successfully completing each task, it provides you with a broader understanding and should be read.

Finally, you will find the INSTRUCTIONS, a walk-through of what to do and when to do it, with illustrations of the key steps and input from the experts to point you toward those little tricks and hints that are the difference between a job well done and a spinal cord injury.

As a closing thought, a note of caution is in order.

Every time you may have tried something new and a little out there, you were asked to read a disclaimer and sign a waiver form. (Truly, the document should be called the "If I Die, It's My Own Damn Fault" form, but that's neither here nor there.)

Most of the things in this book are outlandish. Some are silly perhaps. Quite a few of them, if attempted, may result in a person being shot, killed, maimed, or thrown in jail for a *very* long time. At least two of them include the risk of being eaten by a large animal, and one may place the participant in the clutches of aliens with a predilection for human vivisection.

In retrospect, it would have been appropriate to include a waiver form as part of this book and require you to sign it before you read. Obviously that is impractical; however, in our defense, the author and publishers of this book are not advocating anyone attempting any of the things contained herein. They are simply presented for your information, to answer the simple question—"How would I do that?"

So, please be careful. And whatever you do try, don't try this at home.

DON'T TRY THIS AT HOME

CONDUCT A SWAT-TEAM HOSTAGE RESCUE

What You Will Need

• Two hostage negotiators with throw-phone—a dedicated, hard-wired telephone that can be delivered to the hostage-takers (literally by throwing it) if no other means of secure communications is available.

• One sniper team (one sniper, one spotter) with sniper rifles (SIGARMS Blaser R93 .300 caliber or the EDM Arms Windrunner .50 caliber, for example), scopes, and ammunition

• One hostage rescue team (HRT), six–ten members

• One breaching team (two–four specialists in making openings)

• Battle Dress Uniform (BDU) clothing and web gear (an equipment harness made of nylon straps or "webbing"), soft-soled boots (Tac Boot by Rocky or Fort Lewis Go Devils by Danner), balaclava, all in black

• Type 3 Kevlar body armor (add reinforcing ceramic plates if you suspect rifles or automatic weapons are present), Kevlar gloves, ballistic eye protection (Gargoyles), ballistic helmet

• Heckler & Koch (H&K) MP-5 submachine gun (suppressors optional)—carry four 30-round magazines

• H&K USP .45-caliber handgun with extra magazines

• Flash-bangs (stun grenades)

• Smoke grenades and tear gas

• Two-way radios, including throat mikes and earpieces (use a secure unit that scrambles transmission)

• Fiber-optic video camera—a low-profile camera system that allows you to insert a small, unobtrusive camera into a room or space through a small opening (under a door, for example) and scan a room without being seen.

• Flashlight

• Doorstops, nylon straps (use one-inch tubular weave), knee pads, handcuffs, pepper spray, knife (switchblade recommended), personal first-aid kit

• Canteen and water

• Optional: night-vision equipment (for nighttime or areas with poor lighting and visibility)

⏰ Time Required

Varies, depending on gathering the teams at the site, the situation, and the time for appraisal and planning/rehearsal. Assume a minimum of 90 minutes to a maximum of 48 hours.

☞ Background

General policy within the U.S. law enforcement and military community is that the demands of the hostage-taker are not met. It is felt that doing so only encourages others to take similar actions.

Special training is provided to select individuals in the Federal Bureau of Investigation (FBI) and local law enforcement in hostage rescue and supporting skills. In the case of most agencies, this is covered by the Special Weapons and Tactics (SWAT) teams. Frequently these teams are involved in difficult or exceptional situations, those in which the high level of training is required.

Hostage rescue is one of the more difficult and dangerous challenges for a SWAT team. In these scenarios, a large group of specialists is brought in, including hostage negotiators, sniper teams, breaching teams (specializing in making openings), and the assault team(s). In a perfect setup, all these people will be in place quickly, ready to go. However, these situations are dynamic and do not follow scripts. The ability to apply training and judgment to adapt to the conditions is essential.

In our scenario, approximately ten hostages are being held in the customer service offices of a major software company by an unidentified group of domestic terrorists. Contact with the terrorists has been limited to a patrol officer being warned to keep away. The building is two stories with an office lobby in front and a loading dock and maintenance area in the rear. There is also roof access to the building.

3

 **Instructions**

I. CONTROL THE PERIMETER AND ASSEMBLE YOUR TEAM

Before the SWAT team arrives on the scene, the situation has been identified and patrol officers have established a perimeter around the incident area, approximately 300 yards away from the building. All civilians are being kept back from this area.

Have patrol officers begin collecting intelligence on the situation. Identify the location of all utilities (water, gas, electric) and the shut-off points for the building where the hostages are being held. Contact the building's owner and gather detailed information about the layout, access points, the direction doors swing, etc. If multiple or alternate access points (back doors, roof hatches, etc.) exist, identify their location and configuration. If photographs, videotapes, or blueprints and plans of the building are available, get them. Best of all, if there are any active surveillance cameras or web-cams in the building, get access to them. These will be of invaluable assistance. If the cameras can pan or tilt, leave them as close to their original location as possible to avoid tipping the terrorists off that you are watching them.

Contact the telephone company and have the telephones to the building "locked down" and linked to a phone or phones you designate. By locking the phone down, you will isolate the terrorists from any contact except with you, unless they have cell phones or radios. You can hold the throw-phone for emergencies (such as the regular phone line getting cut).

The members of your SWAT team are on call and carry

their equipment with them, so it will take minimal time to assemble the complete team. However, some delay is possible. Confer with the on-site tactical commander and establish a quick response plan based on your available team and resources. In the event of a life-threatening situation developing rapidly, the available members of the team must be prepared to take immediate action.

2. COMMENCE NEGOTIATIONS

The first step in the hostage rescue is to talk to the terrorists. Hostage negotiation is a skill combining an understanding of the psychology and behavior of the hostage-taker(s) and their motivations with a degree of gut feel for the situation. Your negotiator will contact the terrorists, calling in on a telephone in the building or through the throw phone. His first efforts will be to resolve the crisis without the use of force or loss of life, if possible, and without conceding to any demands.

3. PLANNING AND REHEARSAL

During the negotiation, finish collecting information on the situation, with real-time updates from the negotiator and other sources, and plan the rescue.

In the planning stage of the hostage rescue, five elements are considered:

• The situation: What has happened? While it might seem obvious, the conditions of the hostage situation are essential. You need to understand who the hostage-takers are, how many of them there are, and if they have injured or killed anyone. This, taken with the field conditions, will define much of your approach. A smaller SWAT team may be used for only one or two terrorists. If the access to the building is tight, limiting mobility at any one point, you may choose to insert two teams simultaneously.

• The mission: What does the SWAT team need to accomplish, beyond rescuing the hostages? Are there other elements of concern, such as hazardous materials or an explosive device? If so, planning may need to include an Explosive Ordinance Device team (the bomb squad) or Hazardous Materials (Haz-Mat) team.

• The execution: What is the plan for rescuing the hostages? This is going to depend on the terrain, the number of hostage-takers and their weapons and frame of mind, the hostages, etc. No two situations are going to be exactly the same, and the situation may change during the rescue, so flexibility is essential. In the case of this rescue, the execution will be based on drawing the terrorists' attention toward the front of the building while the SWAT team makes an unobserved entry through the rear.

• Administration/logistics: What materials and resources are needed and what is available? The situation may require a number of different items, from a hostage phone to special listening equipment. Make sure you know what you need before you start.

• Command and communication: Who is in charge, and how will orders and reports be handled? It is essential that the control structure be clear, to avoid any confusion in orders. Miscommunication costs lives. A tactical commander will have overall direction and may order a withdrawal, but the SWAT team leader, *you,* bears responsibility for the rescue once it starts.

It is essential for everyone to understand all of these elements to avoid confusion once the operation begins.

Based on the information available, develop the rescue plan. One of the first decisions to make is whether the rescue will be quiet and stealthy, or rapid and loud. If the layout of the building and the resources allow, you may choose to make a quiet entry. This is done best when you can move to the building unobserved and gain access in a spot the hostage-takers are unlikely to be watching. Roof access hatches, below-ground entries, and other similar points are good choices. Most hostage-takers will focus on front or back doors.

Given the situation, a diversion and a stealthy entry are the best approach. Supporting patrol officers will make a feint at a main entry to distract the terrorists while the assault team moves in from another direction.

Once the plan has been developed and rehearsed to your satisfaction, prepare your team. Your sniper team will select a spot of their own choice, where they can see the scene and gather intelligence on the conditions, which they will relay back to you. If possible, they will choose a spot that allows them to take out terrorists should this become necessary. Sniper teams operate in pairs, with one person acting as the shooter while the other works as a spotter and protects the sniper.

The assault team should assemble and suit up, as should the breaching team.

4. DISCREET MOVEMENT

Move your team to the jump-off point as unobtrusively as possible. Keep journalists from observing your approach and deployment. A marine colonel in the intelligence-gathering business once said that CNN was a great source of information about what his enemy was up to. Don't forget that terrorists and hostage-takers may have a portable television, radio, or cellphone contact with people watching or listening to the news. Do not assume that cutting the power or communication lines causes a total information blackout for the terrorists.

Approach in a way that provides maximum concealment from the terrorists and others. The rule is easiest approach with maximum cover, with an alternate path if available. Always keep your line of retreat in mind and open. Advance in single file with three-paces separation between each team member.

When you have reached the jump-off position (your initial entry point into the building), stack the assault team. Line up tightly and in single file, with your H&K MP-5s ready with the safeties off. As the number one man in the stack, you will be in the front. Reach behind you and squeeze the thigh of the number two man. He or she will pass the squeeze to the next teammate, who will do the same, until the squeeze has been passed all the way to the last in the stack. This is to ask if each team member is ready. The last member in line will squeeze the shoulder of the teammate ahead of him, indicating a go to proceed, which then gets passed forward. Once this reaches you, you will enter the building.

Line the team up as shown. Each team member should confirm
his readiness by squeezing the thigh of the man behind him.

5. DIVERSION, ASSAULT, AND THREAT NEUTRALIZATION

Enter the building through the designated door or access point.
As the team enters a new room, cover and clear the space. Each
team member covers a portion of the room to check for terrorists, hostages, or unusual conditions.

When you approach the area with the hostages, use your
fiber-optic camera to look into the room and assess the situation, noting the location of the terrorists and hostages.
Communicate this to your team through hand gestures and
contact the tactical commander, informing him of your readiness, to make a last check to proceed, and, assuming a go, initiate the diversion. This will begin a 60-second countdown to
detonation of a flash-bang smoke grenade at the front entry of
the building. Be prepared to throw your own flash-bangs into
the area with the terrorists as soon as diversion at the front door
begins.

As soon as the diversion begins, throw or roll two flash-bangs into the room. As they detonate, enter the room with your team rapidly. Shout "GET DOWN" repeatedly. The hostages will drop to the floor.

Your team members will identify and target the hostage-takers. You must determine quickly if they are a threat or not. If they appear to offer surrender, keep them targeted and be prepared to shoot until they are disarmed, facedown on the floor, and subdued with handcuffs.

If the terrorists seem intent on resisting you, threaten a hostage, or appear to draw a weapon, shoot them. Shoot for body mass, two shots minimum, unless you have reason to believe they are wearing body armor. If so, aim for the head. The mantra repeated by SWAT team members is "Two in the chest, one in the head, makes a bad guy good and dead."

Disarm and subdue any terrorists, and make sure that you have accounted for all of them. Hostages may be able to confirm that all terrorists are present or note when one or more left the area. If there are terrorists missing, other officers will enter the scene to take control of the terrorists and hostages, escorting them from the building while you sweep the area.

IMPORTANT NOTE

It is unlikely, but nevertheless possible, that an apparent hostage may in fact be a terrorist. Be sure to account for all guns and identify all persons. The members of the SWAT team should not lower their weapons or ease up until they are comfortable that the situation is completely under control.

Once the situation is under control with patrol officers handling the scene, the SWAT team may stand down and leave the site for a debriefing.

TOW AN ICEBERG TO A DROUGHT-STRICKEN NATION

What You Will Need

- One Mobile Ice Tow System (MITS)
- Three remotely operated vehicles (ROVs)—robotic mini-subs equipped with manipulator arms and color video cameras
- Several thousand square meters of waterproof, fiber-reinforced plastic—a commercial tarp manufacturer will be able to provide this to order.
- Six ocean-going tugboats, each with radio, radar, and eight-person crews—ships and crews can be hired through a commercial ship-leasing agent or one of the major salvage companies.
- Towlines (30–40,000 feet of wire rope, two–four inches in diameter)—typically these will be provided by the tugboat owners.
- Technical team, including three ROV operators, two ROV technicians, six professional scuba divers, and five–seven general support staff

- One drain kit—three three-inch, remotely operated valves, three 500-foot lengths of three-inch fire hose, and three water pumps
- Scuba equipment, including dry suits, buoyancy-control devices, air tanks, fins, masks, weights, underwater lights, and miscellaneous gear
- Waterproof explosives and detonator cord—you will need a permit to purchase these.
- Air compressor for the scuba tanks
- Access to imagery provided by a polar-orbiting observation satellite—available off the Internet.
- Duct tape

Time Required

Three months.

Background

Towing icebergs can serve several purposes. They can be removed from shipping lanes and beached where they pose no threat to navigation. There is a market for glacial water due to its purity and age. For humanitarian reasons, though, it is better to use your ice supply for drought relief.

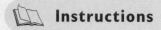 **Instructions**

I. SPOT AND CATCH YOUR BERG

Locate one iceberg.

The ice sheets and glaciers of Antarctica calve off approximately 1,250 cubic kilometers of icebergs each year. Some of the bergs are as large as the state of Rhode Island, which is far too large for this project. Look for a berg about 1,500 feet square. It will extend as deep as 500 feet below the surface and 100 feet above. In rough numbers, it will contain 30 million tons of ice, or 7.5 *billion* gallons of water. (As big as that sounds, it's only enough water for the city of New York for five days.)

When looking for the berg, concentrate on favorable locations that will allow you to work and move the berg easily. The Wendall Sea, just below South America, combines good iceberg hunting grounds with currents that will carry the berg in the right direction.

Use your MITS to approach the berg and set tow points. The number of points will depend on the size of the berg and the type of anchors you use. The best approach is to be overly conservative and install more tow points than you've calculated you'll need. This will benefit you if you hit rough weather, as the strain on the tow points will increase, and more points means a better distribution of the load.

Set the anchors so that they are at a 90-degree angle from the direction of pull. Otherwise you'll pull them loose.

2. WRAP IT UP

The entire point of catching and towing an iceberg is to get the water—as much of it as possible. The iceberg is going to remain largely intact as long as it is in the cold waters of the Antarctic seas—icebergs there have been known to last two years and more. As soon as you start towing the berg into warmer seas it will begin to shed mass as it melts. You need to capture as much of the water as possible. To do this, you will wrap the berg up with the plastic material.

Wrap from the bottom, so that you create a cup under the berg to catch the freshwater as it melts. Examine the underwater portions of the berg with your ROVs, and remove any sharp

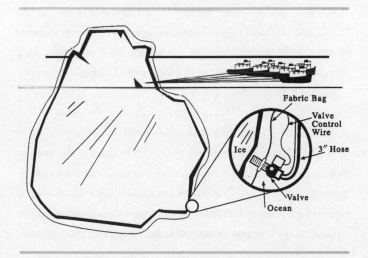

Install drain valves. Pump out any saltwater and periodically check the water for saltiness. Salt content indicates a leak.

edges or pointed sections using explosives. Then position the plastic using your tugs and the ROVs. Multiple wraps, two minimum, are recommended, and any seams below the waterline should be avoided. If they cannot be avoided, have your divers seal the shallow parts and the ROVs handle the deeper sections. Where the anchors are encountered, cut holes through the wrap and seal around them with waterproof tape or hydraulic cement.

You will also install the three-inch valves at this time, setting them into the plastic. One should be at the lowest point on the berg, and the other two 50 and 100 feet below the surface on the flank of the iceberg.

You will use the valves to drain off any saltwater you captured when you first wrapped the ice and to extract it as you make your passage. Use the low valve initially and the higher valves later. If you do get saltwater mingling with the fresh meltwater, the former will tend to be on top as it is lighter. You should use the valves to check how "sweet" the water is on a regular basis.

3. SET YOUR TOW LINES AND MOVE OUT

Now that the berg is wrapped, connect tow lines to the anchor points, preferably by wrapping the berg around the back side to provide more security during the tow. Four tugs will pull, and two will push from behind. Radio contact between the tugs is critical, as is close monitoring of radar.

4. RIDE THE CURRENTS

Pull the berg north from the Wendall Sea and catch a ride east on the Antarctic Circumpolar current. You'll skirt along the southern edge of the Indian Ocean using less engine power and fuel this way.

IMPORTANT NOTE

Remember to have your ROVs and divers check the berg below the waterline on a regular basis to look for and seal leaks and tears. And don't forget to check the meltwater frequently. A salty taste indicates a leak.

Ride the Antarctic Circumpolar current east, gently pushing the berg north as you begin to near Australia. At the eastern edge of the Indian Ocean, you'll catch another current, the South Equatorial, which circulates counterclockwise in the Indian Ocean. It will carry you north and west. Be careful, though. If you go too far north, you'll hit a countercurrent closer into shore from the South Equatorial, and it will push you back to the east and south. Your tugboat captains will use global positioning system (GPS), weather, and real-time oceanographic information provided to them through commercial services that assist in this.

As you approach Africa, head for the drought-stricken nation of your choice.

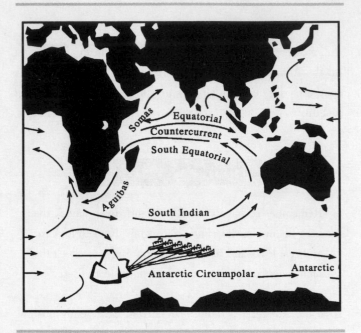

Follow the prevailing current east toward Australia,
then catch the South Equatorial current north and west to the
drought-stricken country of your choice.

BREAK INTO FORT KNOX

What You Will Need

• Assault team totaling ten individuals, all with military experience. Team must include four with reconnaissance and shadowing experience.

• An outgoing personality

• Jaycor electrified water stun guns—avoid lethal weapons.

• Black clothing, including balaclavas, web gear for carrying tools and miscellaneous material, and soft-soled boots—available from an army surplus or security equipment supplier

• Black, lightweight ballistic body armor (helmets are also recommended)—also available at an army surplus store or through mail order

• Latex gloves

• Three cattle trucks, one driver per truck

• One truck loaded with Holstein cows

• One truck loaded with 24 bales of hay

• Two white vans with no rear or side windows

• Two-way, short-range spread-spectrum radios, preferably with scrambling capabilities—available from a security equipment supplier

• Night-vision goggles (avoid surplus Russian military models—there is some evidence that they emit dangerous levels of energy that may cause brain damage).

• Two digital video cameras with tripods, extra recording cartridges, and batteries

• Digital cameras

• One push boat (a type of tug used to push cargo barges on the Mississippi), rusty and well-used with one barge loaded with wheat—arrange lease or purchase through commercial ship-broker.

• One Panamanian-flagged freighter with false hold—arrange lease through commercial ship-broker.

• Five-mil clear plastic sheeting

• Duct tape

 Time Required

Allow three to four months for preparation and obtaining materials. Allow no more than two hours on site at the Depository, from initial contact with the guards to the time you depart with the gold. In terms of post–break-in time, plan on the rest of your natural life being spent outside the United States, preferably in a country that has no extradition treaties with the United States

(Cuba, for example), or a country that will refuse to extradite you in exchange for a percentage of the gold.

☞ Background

The gold at Fort Knox isn't actually at the Fort itself. In fact, the gold is stored at the U.S. Bullion Depository on property that was once part of the Fort's grounds. The Depository consists of a two-story basement and an attic building rising 42 feet above ground. It is built largely of granite, steel, and concrete. Within the building is a two-level steel and concrete vault divided into multiple compartments. The vault door weighs over 20 tons, and for security no one individual knows the combination. To pass through the door, two or more members of the Depository staff must dial in separate combinations. This is going to be the biggest single challenge to overcome.

The vault casing is steel plate, I-beams, and steel cylinders laced with hoop bands and encased in concrete. The vault roof is of similar design and is separated from the Depository roof, as is the outer wall of the vault. The outer wall of the Depository is concrete-lined granite reinforced with steel. There is a front and a rear entry, the rear one being used to receive bullion and supplies. For self-sufficiency, the Depository has its own emergency power plant and source of water.

At the building's exterior, there are four guard boxes at the outer edge of the building, sentry boxes at the entrance gate, and a steel fence surrounding the outer perimeter. In from that is a concrete barrier designed to stop a moving vehicle. The guards work for the U.S. Treasury, and you should assume that they are armed and capable of defending themselves. As an added measure of protection, the complex is monitored and protected with electronic security systems.

As a final and significant level of protection, the soldiers at the Fort adjacent to the Depository are members of the U.S. Army's armored cavalry and are equipped with tanks and armored personnel carriers.

The exact amount of gold in the Depository is debatable. Estimates range from under 1,000 to over 8,500 tons. In terms of dollar value, at $300 per ounce, that means there is between $9.6 billion and $81.6 billion in the vault. The gold is stored in bars measuring 7 inches by 3⅝ inches by 1¾ inches. Each bar weighs approximately 27.5 pounds and is worth $132,000. They are stored unwrapped.

There are three basic ploys to tackling this particular project. First, there is simple brute force—storming the Depository with a team of armed mercenaries. Given the proximity to the Fort itself, it would probably require a full military strike force, including tanks and helicopter gunships to pull this off. In this case, multiple deaths are highly likely and the chances of escape are essentially nil.

The second option is that presented in the James Bond film *Goldfinger*. That plan involved a woman named Pussy Galore and a squadron of specially equipped light aircraft nerve-gassing the facility. The idea is far too cinemagraphic not to attract attention.

The final option is the use of wits and a large dose of coercion. This is the method used in this scenario.

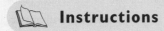 **Instructions**

I. DATA COLLECTION

The Depository is well built and well designed to thwart attempts to break through the walls or sneak past the guards. The systems are too good, the structure too tough. Therefore, the weak link in the security of the gold is the people.

Begin with observation. Set up the digital cameras in covered locations (use the plastic sheeting and duct tape to weatherproof them) to observe the activities of the Depository staff over a period of 96 hours. Remember to change the batteries and recording cartridges regularly. Note the rotation of staff and the license-plate numbers of their vehicles.

Using the services of several private investigation (PI) services, get names and addresses for the staff based on their license plates. Do not ask any single PI service to check on more than three license-plate numbers and mix in random license-plate numbers to avoid making anyone suspicious.

As you receive names and other details of the Depository staff, run credit checks and look for financial difficulties, such as late payments on bills on a regular basis, credit cards that are at their maximum, repossessions, etc. This will provide a point of leverage for future discussions.

Assign members of your team to shadow the Depository staff after hours, particularly those who appear to have some financial problems. Your team should get photographic evidence of any behavior that may be used to help persuade Depository staff to assist you. Adulterous liaisons, use of controlled substances, financial problems, gambling problems, and other personal difficulties are useful to this end.

Also use this preliminary time to scout the area. Identify a point along the Ohio River where you can dock your barge and push boat and dispose of items in the water.

2. CREATE INFLUENCE

Once you have determined the most vulnerable members of the Depository staff, arrange to intercept them while they are off duty, preferably in a situation where you would both have a reason to be—a local tavern, a golf driving range, in the park. It should be someplace you can initiate a casual conversation.

Your goal is to establish a degree of trust and kinship with individuals at the Depository. Pay specific attention to staff such as security officers who know access codes or guards who are in a position to disable other members of the security team. With luck and a friendly enough nature, you can use one or two good contacts to be introduced to others. An outgoing personality is a plus in this case.

Over time, emphasize your concern for these people, become interested in their personal situations and problems, and use this to gently guide them toward introducing the idea that the solution to all their problems may be found somewhere in the vaults. Once they reach a point of comfort with you, they'll probably joke about it. At this point, you have their trust, and you can begin the next stage, establishing the presence of moles (operatives who are trusted within an organization but are working for an outside entity) inside the Depository.

3. INFILTRATION

Now you have reached the point of introducing the idea of re-moving the gold with the help of Depository insiders. Approach the most receptive ones individually—limit these to no more than five people. More than this increases the risk of being found out. In the event of an individual declining or making any hint that they are likely to turn you over to the police, provide them copies of any compromising information you have. If this fails, stun them and tie them up, secreting them in a safe location.

Once insiders have bought into your plan, it is even more essential that you keep an eye on them. Your team should arrange to plant telephone bugs and listening devices in their homes and vehicles. Covert observation is also advised. At the first hint of betrayal, head for the border.

If all goes well, plan the assault for a moonless, rainy night when your moles are on duty.

4. APPROACH AND TAKE CONTROL

Prior to the assault, station the cattle trucks near the Depository at a highway rest stop. All the cattle should be in one truck and 24 bales of hay in another. Your assault team should enter the vans and suit up and test all equipment. No team member should leave the vans until the actual assault begins.

After dark, at a prearranged time, approach the Depository and secrete the vans. Your insiders will neutralize guards, using stun guns you have provided and deactivate the alarm system. Any outside sentries will be knocked out by your assault team. Secure all prisoners with duct tape and gags (making sure they can still breathe adequately) and disable all telephones, radios, computers, and weapons. For hard-wired telephones, cut the cord and smash the handset. For computers and radios, smash the units. Weapons should have their ammunition and firing pins removed.

Meet at the rear door of the facility to gain access. Station one member of your assault team at the front and one at the back to keep watch.

IMPORTANT NOTE

It is essential that you have the right group of people to open the vault combinations. This is easily accomplished if they happen to be working with you. If not, you'll need to bring them to the vault door after you control the facility and get them to unlock the doors. You can do this by bribery—offer them an equal share and safe passage out of the country—or through threats.

5. KNOW YOUR LIMITS

Radio the cattle trucks and have them come to the rear entry of the Depository, where you will load the gold. Layer the gold in the bottom of the empty trucks, no more than 1,500 bars, which equals 41,250 pounds or $198 million in gold. Scatter hay over the gold and transfer the cows to these trucks. Limit yourself to one hour of loading time. Longer than this increases the risk of discovery beyond reasonable limits.

Layer the gold in the back of the truck, scattering a layer of hay over the top of it. Load cows into the truck on top of the hay and gold.

IMPORTANT NOTE

Under no circumstances is anyone to leave the site with gold on their person.

6. CLEAN GETAWAY

Head to the Ohio River to meet your push boat and barge. Load all gold into the barge, covering it with wheat. Dispose of all equipment (radios, stun guns, clothing, etc.) in the river, weighing it down. Once loaded, proceed with the barge downriver. Your ultimate destination is New Orleans, where you will transfer the gold and wheat to the Panamanian freighter.

The cattle trucks should continue on toward the southwest. At some point on the route, the drivers are to find an unattended pasture filled with cows and release your cows there. The rancher may be confused, but he will be grateful. Leave the trucks on an abandoned logging or Bureau of Land Management road in the wilderness.

The other members of your team will scatter and make their way to San Miguel on the island of Cozumel, Mexico, to meet the freighter, which will stand offshore beyond the 12-mile limit in international waters. Arrange to ferry the team out to the freighter on local fishing boats. Once you have the entire team, set sail for your final destination.

IMPORTANT NOTE

Once you have made your way safely out of the United States, you may want to consider Form an Independent Nation, p. 128.

SWIM THE ENGLISH CHANNEL

What You Will Need

- Swim goggles (bring spares)
- Swim cap
- Swimming garment—the Channel Swimming Association (CSA) rules allow for a garment, noting that it may not be neoprene or any material that might assist the swimmer in floating.
- Feeding stick with basket for passing food and liquids
- Food and liquids—carried on the pilot boat
- Grease—any type of protective grease is allowed under CSA rules. A mixture of lanolin and petroleum jelly provided by Boots Chemists, Ltd., in Dover, is highly recommended and perhaps just a bit traditional.
- Glow sticks
- One pilot boat, suitable for a Channel crossing, with observer from the CSA and boat crew (captain and deck hand minimum)—arrangements for the pilot boat will be made through the CSA.
- Support team—include your coach, trainer, and a medical technician at minimum.

- Dry clothing
- Towel
- Passport

 Time Required

Aside from training and preparation time, which depend on the individual, allow approximately 16 hours to make the crossing. Please note that the weather on the English Channel can change dramatically, and you should time your swim around periods of good weather, typically in late spring or summer.

Background

It's not entirely certain when the English Channel was first crossed by a swimmer, but it has certainly been going on for well over 125 years. Dozens of people have made the swim, some of them completing it multiple times. At last check, the reigning champion had completed the crossing 32 times.

You can swim the Channel at your own risk if you like, but to be officially recognized for doing it, you must apply to the CSA, which is the official body responsible for documenting all swims. To obtain an information and rules packet, contact them at Channel Swimming Association, Bolden's Wood, Fiddling Lane, Stowting, Ashford, Kent, TN25 6AP, UK. You'll need to be able to prove that you are healthy, capable of the swim, and between the ages of 16 and 55. The details of proof required are provided by the CSA, but in general you'll need a doctor to sign an affidavit certifying your health and condition.

The majority of England-to-France swims start immediately before or after high water at Shakespeare Beach, particularly during the spring tides. The weather is better this time of year, and the periods of slack water are longer. You will get minimal help from the tide, since it runs parallel to the coast and you'll be swimming across it, but with proper planning, a good pilot, and some luck, you won't be hindered by it.

Aside from the dangers of hypothermia, cramps, and drowning, the biggest risk in the Channel is ship traffic. On a typical day, there are over 600 vessels moving through the shipping lanes, plus assorted ferries, hovercraft, and small boats crossing. You will cross a five-nautical mile (nm)–wide channel on the English side for English inshore traffic, followed by a four-nm–wide lane for traffic heading out into the Atlantic. Then there is a one-nm–wide zone that separates the major shipping lanes. After that will be two lanes on the French side, one five-nm–wide for ships headed for the North Sea, and the other a three-nm–wide channel for French inshore traffic. In other words, for 17 of the 18.2 nautical miles of the swim, you'll be swimming against the light.

You need to be aware of this, but do not worry. Your pilot boat carries the responsibility to monitor shipping traffic with radar and bulletins transmitted by the French and English coast guards. The pilot boat may reroute you or have you tread water in the event of oncoming shipping. In a crisis situation, the pilot boat will remove you from the water.

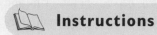 **Instructions**

I. PLAN THE SWIM AND TRAIN

Before you begin your attack on the Channel, you must train for the effort. Not only are you taking on a significant distance (from Shakespeare Beach, Dover, to Cap Gris Nez near Calais is 18.2 nm, or approximately 21 standard miles), you will be doing so in very cold water for an extended period of time. At its warmest, Channel water temperatures may hit 65 degrees Fahrenheit (toward the end of August).

To deal with the distance and the temperatures, set up a training regimen of both distance swimming and cold-water swimming. Your preparation should focus on endurance and the cold. Do not train in warm waters. This will not teach your body to withstand the cold, and your performance will be severely degraded by the Channel's temperatures, impairing your speed and increasing your risk of hypothermia and death.

Gain a modest amount of weight in the form of fat to provide a quick reserve of energy. Eight to ten pounds is a good target. With good training—swimming on an empty stomach—you will teach your body to prey on the fat reserves quickly and efficiently. The added fat will help with buoyancy and heat retention, too.

2. LUBE UP

Before you enter the water, put on your swim garment and apply a coat of grease to your body. The benefit of this includes a small measure of insulation against the cold and a barrier between your skin and the salt water, preventing excess fluid loss from your body and over-absorption of saltwater. It will also prevent stings from jellyfish.

Some portion of your crossing will probably take place in the dark or twilight hours. When this happens, or if the visibility is poor due to fog or rain, attach a glow stick to your suit. These are waterproof and provide good light for several hours. This will make it easier for the pilot boat to keep track of you.

3. SWIM

Proceed to Shakespeare Beach. Get in the water. A CSA representative will note your time of entry. Point yourself in the proper direction (east, and slightly south). Swim.

Individual swimming style is not dictated. Use the stroke or combination of strokes that are most efficient for you. Keep a steady pace and keep moving—this will help you keep warm. Each stroke brings you that much closer to France.

Throughout the swim, pay attention to how you are feeling and your body temperature. If you begin to get too cold, you'll exhibit it in a number of ways, including blue lips or extremities, a lack of feeling in your fingers and toes, and dizziness or disorientation. If this occurs, throw in the towel and climb into the boat. You can try again another time.

4. CARBO-LOAD AND HYDRATE

Given your lack of insulation, it is essential to keep warm. The Channel waters can and will cause hypothermia in the inexperienced swimmer in 30 to 60 minutes. To prevent this, you must keep swimming. Movement keeps your blood flowing and burns calories, helping to maintain core body temperature.

Take regular breaks to eat and drink, once every 30 to 60 minutes. Foods should be high in energy and easily digested. Try plain tofu, which is high in protein, and foods high in carbohydrates, but particularly eat those containing natural sugars, such as apples, bananas, or dried fruits. Be careful, overindulgence will cause gastrointestinal distress. Cornbread or corn muffins are also good. Drink plenty of water and hot liquids (try warmed, diluted Gatorade, for example) to avoid dehydration. Warming the liquids will assist in keeping your body's core temperature up where it needs to be.

IMPORTANT NOTE

By the CSA rules, you may not use any sort of aid in flotation during the swim. This means that while you are allowed to accept food and drink from the pilot boat, you may not touch the boat or any person on it. The standard method of getting your food or liquids is to have it handed over with the feeding stick.

At no time are you allowed to touch the boat or anyone in it. Have the boat crew hand you food and liquids, using a feeding stick.

5. BONJOUR, MON AMI

Under your own power, stagger, crawl, or walk up the beach. Once you touch dry ground above the high-water mark, you've completed the swim and will go into the books. Your only concern at this stage, beyond warming up and toweling off, is to present your passport to the waiting French immigration officials.

FLY THROUGH THE EYE
OF A HURRICANE

What You Will Need

- One WC-130 Hercules aircraft
- Crew: Pilot, copilot, navigator, flight engineer, aerial reconnaissance weather officer, dropsonde system operator (the weather officer and dropsonde operator are optional, but are required if you intend to take weather readings)
- Dropsondes (weather monitoring devices)
- 65,000 pounds of fuel
- One sack lunch and a light snack (fruit, chips, trail mix, etc.)
- Gatorade
- UV-resistant polarized sunglasses
- Dramamine or other anti-motion sickness medications
- Air sickness bag(s)

⏰ Time Required

Allow two to three hours for preflight, six to twelve hours for flight time.

☞ Background

Hurricanes, cyclones, and typhoons are regular events in the Atlantic, Pacific, and Indian oceans and represent the most dangerous and destructive classes of weather in terms of sheer size and force. The areas of the world most likely to spawn these storms are under constant observation by weather satellites, and, when conditions are ripe for trouble, monitoring of the storms moves from satellite to aircraft. In the Atlantic, this is handled by the National Hurricane Center (NHC) in Miami, Florida, which notifies the flight crews.

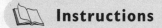 Instructions

I. STAND BY

You can't schedule this. Stand by at your airbase in Florida during the season (August to November). The NHC will track storms crossing the Atlantic from western Africa, watching satellite images for storms that are likely to develop into true hurricanes. They'll call when it's time.

2. BRIEFING AND PREFLIGHT

When a storm reaches the stage that it is a hurricane and thus likely to be a problem, the NHC will call out an order to send your aircraft to fly through it and collect data. The data will be used both to monitor the hurricane in case it decides to get ugly and to further scientific understanding.

You will be briefed on your particular storm, including its location and conditions, the flight plan, and any other pertinent information. This will include data on the hurricane (position, direction of travel, wind speeds), as well as any other important conditions.

An aircraft is simply thousands of parts flying in close formation. After your briefing, walk around the plane, checking for problems—loose wires, leaking lines—anything that might cause the formation of parts to become looser than desired. And be sure to double-check your fuel supply against your flight plan (plus contingency). Aerial refueling is possible with some aircraft, but not in extreme weather conditions.

Complete your preflight checklist and then start the engines. As you start each one, have the dropsonde operator stand by outside the plane, observing the engines. He will report anything unusual, such as flames, vibration, leaking fluids, or excess smoke, which could indicate a malfunction and scrub the mission.

With everyone on board and permission to go from the control tower, proceed to your designated runway for takeoff. With a heavy load of fuel, you will need at least 5,000 feet of runway to get the Herc off the ground.

3. FIGHT OFF BOREDOM

Until you actually get to the hurricane, there won't be much to do. Most of the flying will be done by the autopilot, and, other than checking your course periodically and watching the gauges for any signs of trouble, you've got time to eat lunch, have a cup of coffee, and enjoy the ride. Remember, if you are prone to airsickness, take Dramamine sooner rather than later.

4. BUCKLE UP!

Approach the hurricane from the northwest. About 105 miles from the eye of the storm, descend to 10,000 feet. At this elevation, you will be able to monitor the heart of the storm and release the dropsondes properly once you get to the eye, collecting the most valuable data, while providing a relatively safe flight for your aircraft and crew.

Your weather officer will have been collecting data throughout the flight, but now direct him to switch his instruments to high-density data mode, collecting location and weather information every 30 seconds. All of the information gathered will be transmitted via satellite link back to the NHC for analysis.

The ride is going to start getting really bumpy as the plane fights heavy winds, and visibility will drop to zero. In this situation, you may not even be able to see the tips of the plane's wings. Don't worry. This is typical. As you close on the eyewall (the ring of clouds that surrounds the eye of the hurricane), it will get progressively worse. Make sure you're seated and strapped in before you actually transit the eyewall. Do an intercom check with the crew to ensure they are in their places and secure.

5. THE CALM

The plane will get slapped around pretty badly as you pass through the eyewall. Downdrafts may force the plane to drop as much as 1,000 feet, but, after two to four minutes, the darkness will quickly disappear, the rain scouring at the plane's skin will cease, and you will emerge into the relative calm that is the hurricane's eye. Now you are in the "stadium," flying across a cylinder of clear air, with tier upon tier of clouds like the seats at a sports arena rising up to blue sky and dropping to the ocean's surface two miles below.

Turn up the air conditioning. The eye has a higher temperature than the surrounding clouds, and it will get very warm, 80 degrees Fahrenheit or hotter.

Make sure the dropsonde operator is ready, and head the plane for the center of the eye. As you pass over the center, the operator will load a dropsonde into its launch tube. Your weather officer will monitor the outside wind speeds carefully. Taking into account the airspeed of the plane, he will note that the wind, which was coming from the left, will drop suddenly, then shift to the right.

When this happens, you are in the exact center of the hurricane. Direct the dropsonde operator to release the dropsonde. The unit, about 16 inches long and 3.25 inches in diameter, is ejected from the launch tube and deploys a parachute that allows it to float slowly to the ocean surface below. As it falls, it will monitor outside temperature, humidity, and atmospheric pressure relative to altitude, creating a vertical profile of the storm's eye. The data are transmitted back to the plane using a high-frequency radio, where your operator analyzes it and encodes it for transmission back to the NHC via satellite.

6. X MARKS THE SPOT

Fly through the eyewall on the opposite side of the eye from where you entered it and head out toward the southeast another 105 miles, then turn due north. Using your guidance system, fly 140 miles, then turn to the southwest and head into the eye again. This is the start of what is called an Alpha Pattern, a flight path that looks like a giant X when drawn on a chart of the

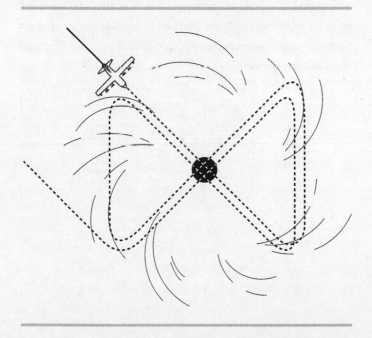

Make four passes through the eye of the hurricane, tracing an X pattern.

storm. The Alpha Pattern brings your plane repeatedly through the heart of the hurricane.

Once you enter the eye, repeat the dropsonde launch procedure, exit the eye, traveling another 105 miles out, then turn north again for another 140 miles, then turn to the southeast through the eye. Follow this pattern until you have passed through the eye a total of four times, which will take about eight hours and is a safe limit for crew fatigue and fuel load.

Four passes is the standard assignment, and after completing the four passes return to the airbase. Another plane will take over monitoring. This level of real-time, continuous monitoring will provide valuable meteorological data to the NHC and the weather services, which can be used to prepare for emergency response to the individual storm, as well as to better understand hurricanes in general.

SALVAGE PART OF THE *TITANIC*

What You Will Need

- One fully rigged deep-water salvage vessel, equipped with rear-deck work areas, multiple cranes and winches, storage lockers for chain, cables, etc., global positioning system (GPS), and bow and stern thrusters to assist in maintaining position over the wreck. The ship must be provisioned for a crew of 30 and the salvage team.
- Two two-person mini-submarines, rated to 20,000 feet, with external robotic arms, with pilots and maintenance team
- Spare parts for the mini-subs
- One submarine tender (a ship specifically designed to maintain and service submarines) with crew
- Two–four remotely operated vehicles (ROVs), capable of operating at 20,000 feet with operators and maintenance crew
- Fifteen lift bags rated to 4,000 pounds of lift each
- Canvas padding material

- Thirty tons of anchor chain—this can be acquired from a marine scrap dealer
- Extra diesel fuel
- EOScan sonar system
- Underwater lighting systems—battery-powered and suitable for 13,000-plus feet
- Underwater signal beacons—acoustical emitters rated for 13,000-plus feet
- Multiple remote-release mechanisms and control system—these can be fabricated by a marine equipment company and must be designed to be activated by a coded acoustical signal.
- One documentary film crew with equipment
- Dramamine

⏰ Time Required

Five weeks, depending on weather and court challenges.

☞ Background

Any object in the water will appear to weigh less than it would on dry land. This is because the weight of the object is decreased by the weight of the volume of water it displaces (about 64 pounds per cubic foot of seawater). To illustrate, assume you have a one-foot-square metal box that weighs 120 pounds on land. When dropped into water it will sink. Once it is in the water, its apparent weight would only be 56 pounds because it displaces one cubic foot of water (which weighs 64 pounds). In order to lift the cube from the bottom, the lift applied to the box must be more than 56 pounds. This is important and is going to make it possible to accomplish this task.

There are a lot of methods for raising something from under the water. One approach is to use brute force, attaching cables to the object and pulling it up with a winch. However, the deeper the object, the more cable you'll need, and you're not only lifting the object, but the weight of the cable. Since the *Titanic* is 12,600 feet down, you'd need a lot of very heavy cable to pull up anything of any size. It could be done, but it's not the most elegant way to manage it.

The second option for raising something is a buoyant lift using pontoons or lift bags. Similar to attaching a helium balloon to a small object, if the lift of the pontoon or lift bag is greater than the weight of the object, it will rise. For a salvage effort in two-plus miles of open ocean, this is the more practical and simple way to manage it.

 Instructions

I. FIND THE *TITANIC*

Up until Bob Ballard located the *Titanic* on September 1, 1985, her exact location wasn't known. Even after he found her, the coordinates were held in some secrecy, but now the great ship's resting place is well documented. Proceed in your salvage vessel directly to 41 degrees 44 minutes north latitude, 49 degrees 55 minutes west longitude.

2. RUN SILENT, RUN DEEP

Once you have reached the general vicinity of the wreckage, proceed in a box-search pattern using sonar to locate its exact location. A box search will involve starting at the coordinates of the wreck and charting a course that describes the four sides of a rectangle, moving farther out from the starting point each time. The ocean floor immediately around the wreck is flat, and the hull of the *Titanic* will stand out as a ridge about 800 feet long. When you spot it, note the coordinates of your ship's position on your charts. Confirm this with your GPS.

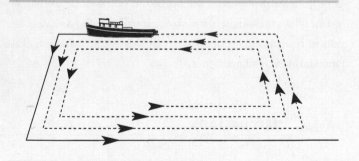

Conduct a box-search pattern, starting at the known location
of the wreck, working your way out from there.

At the wreck's coordinates, launch your ROVs to confirm you are in the right position and to scout the bottom for a salvage target. It is more cost-effective to use the ROVs for this than the manned subs. The ROVs should look for parts of the ship that are either already separated or loose enough to be cut free with minimum effort. The target should also be in good enough condition to survive the salvage and should have some aesthetic appeal. Do not settle for the first slab of plate steel you encounter. It should have some feature that identifies it with the *Titanic* and shipwrecks, such as a porthole or watertight door.

It is important to have an estimate of the object's weight. Allowing for the decrease in weight due to water displacement, this will allow you to estimate the lift required to bring the item to the surface. To determine the weight, estimate the volume of the object from measurements. Multiply the volume by the weight of steel. Steel plating one inch thick weighs approximately 41 pounds per square foot and displaces 5.33 pounds of water. The net lifting force required for a one-square-foot plate of this thickness is about 36 pounds. A solid section of hull plating one inch thick measuring eight feet by ten feet would weigh 3,280 pounds while displacing about 426 pounds of water. The lift applied would need to be in excess of 2,854 pounds.

For purposes of safety, all lifting hardware should be rated to 120 percent of the dry-land weight of the salvage target (in this example, that would be the full 3,280 pounds). This gives a margin of error and takes into account the fact that once the object clears the water at the surface, you will have to move its full weight.

Once your ROVs have identified a good candidate, launch one of your submarines to take a closer look and, assuming the target is good, to mark it with an acoustic signaling device.

3. LIGHT THE ABYSS

At a depth of 12,600 feet, it is utterly black, with the exception of the occasional flash of light provided by bioluminescent sea-life. In order to work effectively, you will need to provide work lighting at the salvage target.

Lower light units with cables to the bottom near the salvage target from the salvage vessel. Once on the bottom and situated properly by your subs, disconnect the cables and retract to the surface. Four to six light units should suffice.

Lower steel cables to the wreck, padding the cable with canvas to keep from damaging the wreckage or the lines. Use the Rule of Three—if one is adequate to do the job, use three. This provides a degree of redundancy that is unlikely to ever fail under normal circumstances. Run several groups of three cables each, determining the total number of and size of the cables to meet safe margins for your weight estimate on the wreckage. Use ¾-inch cables at minimum. Connect and secure each group of three cables to lifting eyes, a reinforced, looped cable end.

IMPORTANT NOTE

When you don't have subs or ROVs active on the bottom, turn off your work lights.

4. OIL AND WATER DO NOT MIX

Once you've prepped the wreckage with cables and lifting eyes, you will prepare to deploy the lift bags. Unlike traditional pontoons, which are reinforced metal tubes filled with high-pressure air, lift bags are soft-sided and filled with diesel fuel from your ship's reserves.

The water pressure at the *Titanic*'s depth is extreme, about 370 times greater than the pressure at the surface. Because of this, the amount of compressed air required to be pumped over two miles down just to prevent the pontoons from being crushed would be tremendous. The pontoons would also have to be extremely rugged to withstand the pressure changes from surface to bottom and back again, especially as they bleed off excess pressure as they ascend. If the pressure inside these types of pontoons gets too high, they will rupture as depth decreases.

Diesel-filled lift bags do not have the same problem. They are soft-sided and filled with a noncompressible liquid, so pressure changes are of no consequence. The diesel fuel is lighter than the surrounding water. No matter the depth, they will lift, and pressure changes will not be a concern.

Fill each bag with diesel fuel at the surface and ballast it with the scrap anchor chain or other waste metal. Each bag will require 4,000 pounds of ballast, plus another 1,000 pounds to make it sink and keep it stable on the bottom. The bags should be equipped with a sonar transponder to make finding them easy should they drift, and the link between the ballast and the bag will require a remote-release device.

Use a crane to raise each bag from the deck of the ship as it is prepped, then lower it into the water and release it.

IMPORTANT NOTE

When you drop the bags over the side, target them, taking into account any drift due to current. Drop them close to, but not directly on top of, the wreckage. Be sure to keep your mini-subs clear of the target area during the dropping of lift bags.

Once the bags are on the bottom, the mini-subs will gather them up and connect them to the lifting shackle. It is highly recommended to connect each one to at least two different sets of lifting shackle, in case one lets go, and to use more bags than you've calculated as necessary. Because water temperature and density varies with depth, it is possible that the bags may stall when they hit a temperature increase—use 20 percent minimum more lifting power than is required.

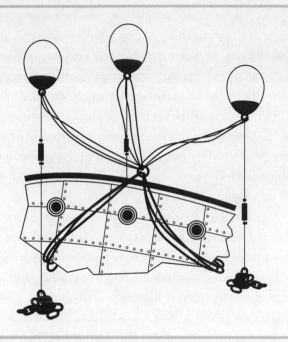

Rig the lifting bags to the wreck with the lifting shackles.
Use more bags than necessary.

In the example given previously, a 3,280-pound steel plate could be easily handled by a single lift bag exerting 4,000 pounds of lift.

5. HEAVE-HO

After completing the fit-out of the lift bags to the wreckage, double- and triple-check the setup, and station the mini-subs near the lift area, close enough to observe, but not so close as to become entangled in the rigging.

Your bags are held in place by the ballast (the anchor chain). The two are connected by your acoustically activated release devices. At your direction, one of the subs at the site will emit a signal pulse from an external transponder. Each of your release devices has a separate activation pulse encoded into it so that you may release the lift bags sequentially. If you've calculated properly, you won't need to drop all of the ballast, which is acceptable. If the wreckage stalls out during ascent due to a temperature inversion or equipment failure, you will drop additional weight.

The surfacing will take two or more hours. Monitor the position and heading of the wreckage and keep your ships clear. Once the bags surface, send divers into the water to rig lines from the crane on your salvage ship to the lifting eyes. Make sure they also rig recovery lines to the lift bags.

Once everything is secure, take up tension on the wreckage and disconnect the bags. Lift the wreckage to the deck and place it in a tank of freshwater. It will begin to corrode quickly now that it is exposed to an oxygen-rich atmosphere, and the freshwater will assist in slowing this, as well as leaching salt out of the wreckage.

6. BE GREEN

Oil is not friendly to sea life, nor is it cheap. Be sure to reclaim the diesel fuel from the lift bags once you've stowed the wreckage. Retrieve your lights as well.

7. DECLARE A LOSS

Salvage of the *Titanic* is allowed as long as any material raised is not sold at a profit. You may choose to use the Hollywood definition of profit (which is, no matter how well the movie does, it didn't make any money), or donate the salvaged material to a worthy beneficiary and take the tax benefit. You might lose money on that, but a good deal with the documentary film crew to broadcast the salvage will offset losses.

WRESTLE AND WIN
A *SUMO* MATCH

What You Will Need

- One *dohyo (sumo* ring)
- One *mawashi* (colored-silk loincloth)
- One or more *rishiki* (opponent)
- One *gyoji* (referee)
- *Chikara-mizu* (sacred water)
- *Chikara gami* (towel)
- *Shiko* (salt)

 Time Required

Training time, plus approximately three to ten minutes per bout, plus two weeks to complete a full tournament.

☛ **Background**

Sumo wrestling dates back many centuries in Japan and has only opened up to non-Japanese in the last few years. As recently as the 1970s, a Hawaiian-American named Jesse Takimiyama was the only foreigner competing. In the 1990s, the top ranks of *sumo* included at least three Americans (Akebono, Musashimaru, and Konishki), all born in Hawaii. Most have taken Japanese citizenship, which seems to make them more palatable to Japanese fans. To be truly successful in *sumo,* you will need to follow this example.

Sumo is not a matter of two fat men in *mawashis* grappling each other. Seventy different wrestling techniques are identified, involving slapping, pushing, lifting, and throws, all based on skill and strength.

There are clear rules. It is forbidden to punch (with a closed fist), gouge the eyes, kick the chest or belly, pull hair, bend fingers back, or slap *both* of your opponent's ears simultaneously. Victory is achieved by forcing your opponent out of the grass-stalk circle marking the inbounds area on the *dohyo,* or forcing the other *rishiki* to touch a portion of his body other than the soles of his feet to the clay surface first.

There are occasions when one wrestler succeeds in throwing the other down, but is pulled over on top of him. In this case, the wrestler on top may extend a hand to break his fall and touch the *dohyo* floor first. He will still be declared the winner, as he was protecting the other wrestler from injury.

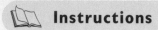 **Instructions**

I. APPRENTICESHIP AND ABUSE

Apply to and become a member of a *sumo* stable. These are run by senior, usually retired, wrestlers. You will be required to act as a servant for the senior stable members, and much of your time will be spent cleaning, cooking, and running errands for them. Over time, you will be taught techniques and be used as a sparring partner in practices.

This experience can be humiliating, but is an important part of the process. You will learn valuable lessons and develop a sense of calm and cool that are characteristic of *sumo*. When you're ready to compete, you'll be told by your trainers.

2. BULK OUT AND BUFF UP

There is no ideal size for a *sumo* wrestler. In the last few decades, weights have climbed, with the largest wrestlers competing weighing in excess of 500 pounds. A 250-pound wrestler is considered small. A good target weight is 325 to 375 pounds, which is sufficient size without losing speed and agility.

The basic *sumo* diet should be high in carbohydrates and designed to add bulk. Combine this with an exercise regimen focusing on speed, strength, and flexibility. Exercise caution in your weight gain, and work out. Excess weight on a lighter bone structure will lead to permanent damage to your knees, hips, and ankles. Swimming and in-water exercises serve to build aerobic fitness and strength in a low-impact environment. Set up a regular routine of weight-lifting and practice bouts against other wrestlers.

3. THE *BASHO*—TOURNAMENT TIME

Sumo competitions are called *bashos* and typically run over a 15-day cycle. Each wrestler will compete once a day, unless injured and incapable of continuing.

When you enter the *dohyo* to compete, flex your muscles and stamp your feet, raising each leg as high as you can and bringing it down hard (this is called the *shiko* and serves to both stretch your muscles and intimidate your opponent). Then rinse your mouth with *chikara-mizu* (a ladle filled with the water will be handed to you by the *rishiki* who wrestles next), and wipe your lips with a *chikara gami* (a special paper towel). This will serve to cleanse the spirit.

Keep a straight face—no smiles, no hint of emotion.

Face into the ring from your corner and cast your *shiko* (salt) to the center. The cast should be smooth, high, and hard, emblematic of your flexibility and strength. Some wrestlers add a touch of flamboyance to the throw, which many fans love.

Psychological warfare is part of *sumo,* and different wrestlers take different approaches to it. Some prefer to be utterly focused and stoic, as though their opponent is a small obstacle to be pushed aside. Others use the casting of salt to show off and intimidate. The most aggressive wrestlers will pause momentarily after throwing their salt and briefly eyeball the other *rishiki.* A long, hard stare in *sumo* borders on trash talk.

Your approach to this is entirely up to you and in keeping with your personality.

4. *SHIKIRI*

Approach your line in the *dohyo*. Continue to stare at the other wrestler and squat down, leaning forward and supporting yourself with your fists. This process is the *shikiri*. As you lean forward, keep your eyes focused on the other wrestler, watching his hands and eyes. By gauging each other's body language and expression, you must decide to start or not. Both *rishiki* must be ready. If neither you nor the other wrestler feels the moment is right, step back to your corner, cast more salt into the ring, and resume the position. Three to four minutes are allowed for this cycle in each bout, depending on the division you are in.

Approach your line in the *dohyo*, lean forward, and place your fists on your line. Maintain eye contact with your opponent throughout.

When you are ready, take a deep breath, and explode up and off your line in the *tachi-ai* (the initial charge). Judge your timing carefully, and watch your balance and speed. Too fast a *tachi-ai* against a smaller, faster wrestler will allow him to side-step or leapfrog over you.

IMPORTANT NOTE

Breath control is critical. You should be able to conclude the match without taking a second breath. Otherwise, you lose strength.

The most successful techniques used in *sumo* are *yorikiri,* the frontal force-out, and *oshidashi,* the frontal push out. If you employ *yorikiri,* grab the other wrestler's *mawashi* and lift him out of the ring. If you prefer *oshidashi,* push him out using your mass and speed. If you are outweighed by your opponent, try the sidestep or leapfrog. Do not employ consistent techniques; this will make you predictable.

Once you have come to grips, keep pressing and pushing. Do not let go, and force the other wrestler out of the *dohyo,* or off his feet. As soon as he is down, stop.

5. GRACE AND POISE

Upon winning your bout, do not smile or celebrate. Any excessive displays are frowned upon by the fans. Instead, help your opponent up if it is reasonable to do so, accept your victory with good grace, and retire to the locker room.

FIND AND CATCH
THE LOCH NESS MONSTER

What You Will Need

- Scuba-diving gear with Nitrox breathing gases
- Scuba-phone underwater communication system
- Jonlines (loops of rope secured to the underwater line that prevent you from drifting)
- One dive-support boat
- One trawler with nets and winches
- One large holding tank
- Six cabin cruisers equipped with side-scanning sonar and low-light underwater video imaging systems—arrange to lease these from a broker in Inverness, Scotland.
- Underwater lights—these are available from a commercial diving company.
- Underwater dart guns and several hundred cubic centimeters (cc) of concentrated Ketamine, a sedative known to work on reptilian nervous systems
- One acoustic signal device, also fitted to a dart gun

- One marine biologist—contact the University of Edinburgh for a reference.
- One large-animal vet, preferably with experience with large marine animals
- Chum—a mixture of animal or fish blood and entrails
- Live bait

🕐 Time Required

Allow two to three weeks prep time, and anywhere from one to five days for tracking and netting.

☞ Background

Loch Ness is a long freshwater lake that sits between the Scottish Highlands and the "South," as it is called with just a tinge of disdain by highlanders. The loch was formed in a low spot caused by a combination of fault lines and glaciers. The resulting body of water is over 700 feet deep, cold, and has the coloration of very strong Earl Grey tea.

The Loch Ness monster, Nessie, has been sighted for centuries, and "documented" in photographs that remain controversial. Given the statements of the size, shape, and behavior of the monster, many experts suggest that, if she exists, Nessie would probably be a plesiosaur, an ancient marine animal growing up to 50 feet in length and thought to have died out some 65 million years ago.

Proving her existence is problematic, lacking solid evidence. Some scientists have tackled the question of Nessie from a very simple point of view—diet. An animal approaching the size of a plesiosaur would have a prodigious appetite. Loch Ness, like many Scottish lakes, is a particularly poor body of water, and studies have shown that there is not adequate food in the lake to support a healthy breeding population of plesiosaurs. However, it is still possible she exists.

 Instructions

I. LEARN TO BE STILL

Your operational plan is straightforward. Find Nessie, then stun and capture her.

Sightings have been scattered around the Loch, and there's no promise that any of them are reliable. Using her need to eat as a starting point, work in the northeastern end of the Loch near the village of Lochend, where surveys show a more productive and healthy food chain. Like stalking land-based game at a water hole, it makes more sense to wait for Nessie in an area where she is most likely to appear.

Be very patient.

2. ANCHOR AND PREPARE THE EQUIPMENT

Anchor your dive-support boat in a depth of approximately 150 feet of water. The boat should lower a weighted line to a depth of 75 feet. This will be the location you and the other divers will work from. Position the cabin cruisers at even intervals on a circle 400 yards out from the dive boat. Each one should deploy their underwater cameras and sonar at a depth of 75 feet, facing out from the circle.

An additional camera should be suspended 50 feet directly below where you will be waiting, and one more should be in the same general vicinity as you.

Begin releasing the chum into the water.

3. GEAR UP AND ENTER THE WATER

You and the other divers should set up your gear now, being especially sure to double-check your Nitrox gas mix. Nitrox has a higher concentration of oxygen than nitrogen, thus reducing the amount of the latter gas you absorb and allowing more time at depth without fear of decompression sickness. An improper balance of nitrogen and oxygen in your tanks can lead to dangerous situations, including deadly oxygen toxicity. Once you have checked and rechecked, enter the water and descend along the working line to 75 feet. Connect yourself to the line with your Jonline.

The cabin cruisers will monitor visually and acoustically for the approach of Nessie. Once they've spotted her on sonar, they will relay her direction relative to you and the depth she is approaching from as well as her speed. This will allow you to orient yourself toward her and turn on the underwater floodlights. The advantage of the floods is twofold: first, they will help you see in the otherwise dim waters, and, with the floods aimed away from you and toward the monster, it will make it harder for her to see you, but not vice versa. It should also attract her to your location.

Make sure to take the safety off the dart guns.

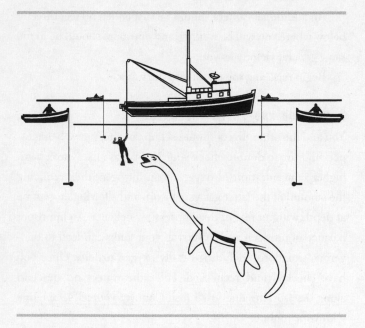

Deploy the dive-support boat with cabin cruisers in a 400-yard-radius circle around it. Lower a work line from the dive-support boat, and descend in your dive gear to a depth of 75 feet.

4. KNOCK OUT, NET UP

As Nessie approaches to within 15 feet, fire both the tranquilizer darts and the acoustic signal device at her, aiming for her underbelly. Typically, reptile skin is thinner and more easily penetrated on this part of the body. This is probably the case for Nessie as well.

It will take a few minutes for the Ketamine to begin to kick in. Given the estimated size of Nessie, approximately 10,000 pounds, it will not be possible to knock her out completely. However, the darts should slow her down significantly. If she leaves the area, the signal from the acoustic device will allow you to track her as she moves away.

Surface slowly (no more than 30 feet per minute), with any decompression stops required.

Signal success to the dive boat and have the cabin cruisers and trawler dispatched to track Nessie. As she slows sufficiently, the trawler will deploy a capture net and haul her up. They must move quickly. Like many air-breathing marine animals, Nessie is probably capable of staying underwater for extended periods, but assume this is no more than five to ten minutes.

Once brought onboard, have Nessie checked over by the vet and marine biologist prior to transfer into the holding tank. You don't want to be known as the person who found and *killed* the Loch Ness monster.

5. CONTACT THE PRESS

Have your press agent contact the *Weekly World News, National Enquirer, New York Times, CNN,* and *60 Minutes* to open the bidding for the exclusive story and interviews. Seven figures, to start.

GO OVER NIAGARA FALLS IN A BARREL

What You Will Need

- One barrel
- Protective clothing, including knee and elbow pads
- Helmet—a climber's helmet or football helmet with face guard will work well.
- Mouth guard—chipped teeth are no fun and will ruin the post-success photos.
- Cell phone or two-way radios with fresh batteries
- Important telephone numbers—weather information: 905-688-1847; Greater Niagara General Hospital: 905-358-0171
- One bottle of good champagne and Waterford crystal glasses—do not take champagne or glasses along in barrel.
- One flatbed truck with medium-duty crane
- Three–five friends
- Representatives of the media and/or someone who knows how to take good pictures
- Bail money

⏰ Time Required

Varies, depending on availability of barrel. Allow no more than 15 minutes to get the barrel in the water and launched (any longer may allow authorities to interfere), and 60 to 90 minutes from launch to retrieval at the other end of the falls.

☞ Background

Niagara Falls is really two falls—Horseshoe Falls on the Canadian side and American Falls on the U.S. side. Horseshoe Falls drops 170 feet into the Maid of the Mist pool. American Falls drops between 70 and 110 feet, but the drop, while shorter, is onto rocks. The best time to run the falls is in the late spring or summer, when more water runs over; otherwise you run the risk of hanging up on one of the many rocks that pepper the river's bottom.

The first recorded and successful trip over the falls was done by a woman, Annie Taylor, in October 1901. Ms. Taylor's barrel was made of wood, but did not look like the conventional image of a wine or beer barrel. Since then, most barrels have been custom-built and have included everything from one fabricated out of two water heaters to a modified diving bell.

The most important point is that it is better to drop farther and miss the rocks. You will be forgiven if your "barrel" resembles something designed for safely transporting raw eggs through a hurricane.

Instructions

I. BUILD A BETTER BARREL

Before you make your attempt to run the falls, you'll need a barrel that can stand the pounding it will take during the run up to the falls and the drop-off. Further, it must be built to protect your life and well-being. You will not be able to buy a barrel of this type anywhere, so manufacturing one is the proper course. The essentials for a good barrel include:

• Build it of ³⁄₁₆-inch reinforced steel, watertight with an access hatch. The hatch should be modeled on the watertight doors on ships, with a rubber seal between the mating surfaces of the hatch and the barrel. The hatch should be secured in place with four–six latches that will not pop on impact, but can be easily opened in an emergency. Above all, the weight of the hatch must not exceed 40 pounds, which is the maximum most people can lift with one arm (this assumes both an emergency and an injury such as a broken arm or collarbone).

• The barrel should be approximately four–five feet in diameter, eight–twelve feet long, with rounded ends to help prevent the barrel from hanging up on rocks. It will resemble an oversized steel beer keg.

• Ballast and a keel are recommended to help stabilize the barrel during the lead-in to the falls and after it lands in the Maid of the Mist pool. The keel should be about three inches deep. Ballast should be in the form of neoprene bags filled with lead shot (the kind used in shotgun shells) affixed to the inside of the barrel above the keel. A modest amount of ballast, no more than 300 pounds, is adequate.

• Include a heavy-gauge viewing window or windows, at least one-inch thick. This can be made of Plexiglas and sealed in with waterproof caulking to prevent leaks.

• A steering apparatus is optional.

• Air supply suitable for 90–120 minutes. This can be supplied by one or two scuba tanks (use high-pressure 80-cubic-foot models pressurized to 3,000 psi) and a scuba regulator. Be sure the tanks are secured and well padded.

• Everything inside the barrel should be secured and strapped down.

• The inside should be padded with soft foam rubber held in place with nylon strapping or duct tape. Pay close attention to the padding on all sharp corners and edges in particular.

• Provide two-inch nylon webbing straps to secure yourself during the trip.

Construction of the barrel can be handled by a welding and machine shop. They will supply all steel and fittings, though you will need to provide the air supply.

Once you have built the barrel, be sure to run it through an unmanned test in real water. Many past barrels have weighed in excess of 1,000 pounds, and a minor or major leak combined with the weight of the barrel causes them to sink.

2. LAUNCH

Transport the barrel as quietly as possible (if the truck can be equipped with removable sidewalls, use them; if not, cover the barrel with a tarp) to the area of the Whirlpool Bridge. Use the truck's crane to quickly lower you and the barrel into the river. Once you are in the water, it will be difficult to stop you, and the only risks are getting hung up on a rock if the water is low or being forced into the bank by catching the wrong current.

3. BUTTON UP AND HOLD ON

Once you are sure of your approach to the Falls, close and secure the hatch. Immediately turn on your air supply and secure

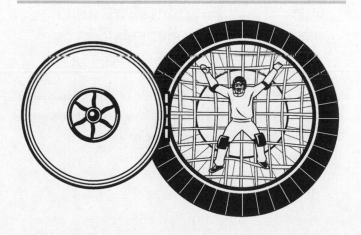

Put on your protective gear and get into the restraining strap web.
Do not arch your back.

yourself in the restraining straps. It is important to cushion your spine against impact, so under no circumstances arch your back. Stay calm and loose.

4. OVER THE EDGE

You'll know when you've gone over. The sound of the Falls will be deafening, and the barrel will fall for approximately three seconds and may tumble in the process. Upon striking the pool below, the barrel may become entirely submerged, depending on its weight. Barring serious damage or a leak, you will rebound to the surface very quickly.

Once you have hit the pool, call your shore crew to let them know you are alive and well. Wait at least five minutes before opening the hatch to allow the barrel to move away from the Falls. Otherwise, you will flood the barrel and sink.

Wait for the authorities or local boaters to retrieve you; alternately, you may wait for the barrel to beach itself.

5. CELEBRATE YOUR CONTINUED LIFE

Step out of the barrel. Take the bottle of chilled champagne from one of your assistants and shake it vigorously. Spray everyone within 15 feet in celebration of being alive.

Surrender to the authorities.

COMPETE IN AND WIN A JOUST

What You Will Need

• One suit of armor

• One sturdy warhorse—breeds such as the Clydesdale are well suited to carrying the extra load that your armor represents. Don't skimp on the horse. You will also need protective armor for your horse.

• A jousting saddle—the saddle will have a high cantle (the back of the saddle), up to one foot tall, to help prevent you from being pushed off.

• Multiple lances with coronal-type tips. The coronal has three tips to spread the impact, reducing injury. The lances should be made from hardwood and be ten–twelve feet in length, depending on your strength and size.

• Optional: Sword or other handheld weapons and shield. Should you compete in other events or be required to defend yourself on foot once unhorsed, you will need a sword. Odds are against you when fighting afoot with a mounted knight.

• One squire and one additional attendant to assist in suiting up, setting the saddle on your horse, and adjusting equipment and weapons

IMPORTANT NOTE

Many of the items you will need are not commonly available. Your armor and weapons should be custom-made for your body. To find an armorer, contact your local medieval re-enactment organization, such as the Society for Creative Anachronism.

⏱ Time Required

Allow one hour prep time, ten minutes for the joust.

☞ Background

Jousting started during the medieval era in Europe as a way of practicing the arts of noble combat in a relatively safe venue. Jousting was typically the main event in most tournaments of arms at this time and required two knights in armor mounted on horses to charge one another along a separating wall (called a tilt barrier). Both knights held blunt-tipped lances designed to knock the other off his horse without killing him.

Jousting is the official sport of the state of Maryland.

 Instructions

I. SUIT UP

Get a suit of armor. Jousting armor is significantly different from the armor used in real combat. It is highly specialized to address the particular needs of the event. For example, your jousting armor should be rounded, heavier on the left side than on the right (the side most exposed to lance blows), and well padded on the inside to reduce injury and impact. A shield may be carried separately in the left hand, or built into the left side of the armor.

At minimum, the armor should use 12-gauge plate steel. Do not use chain mail under any circumstances. Chain mail will catch the point of your opponent's lance and cause severe injury. Padding may be built into the inside of the armor or provided through a separate garment worn under the armor. Three-quarters of an inch of heavy cotton batting inside canvas and cotton duck is sufficient.

To every extent possible, make sure that any openings or places that could catch the point of a lance are as small as possible or covered with a layer of armor to shed the point. Eyeslits on your helm (the proper term for your helmet) will need to be very narrow; the joints in your armor at the shoulder, elbow, neck, and thigh should have curved plate coverings that will de-flect or allow the lance tip to slide off.

Be sure your armor is well polished and oiled, devoid of rust or scratches. Your shield should bear your crest or symbol.

Suit up and test the armor for fit and ease of movement. A light oil may be applied to squeaky joints.

2. SADDLE UP

Jousting armor may weigh 50 pounds or more. It's not as heavy as true battle armor, but you should use a stepladder and/or a boost from your squire to get in the saddle. Make sure your feet are solidly in the saddle's stirrups, and grip the horse's flanks hard with your knees.

Take your lance from your squire, holding it upright with your right arm.

Take your lance from your squire, holding it upright in your right hand.

Say thank you to the squire.

3. ACQUIRE A FAVOR

Find an attractive lady of noble birth, preferably one that you would wish to have positive feelings toward you. Ask her if you might carry her favor. If she agrees, she'll present you with a scarf or some other object, probably of cloth, that you can wear as you joust. By asking for and accepting her favor, you have become her champion, and it would not be good to lose, unless you want her to be humiliated, too. Wear the favor tied prominently about your upper arm.

4. TKO

Once the signal is given, ride hard along the tilt barrier. Do not focus on steering your mount, as the horse is well trained and will follow the wall separating you from your opponent. Spur the horse as appropriate, and focus your attention on your opponent.

Lean forward (this helps keep you from being unseated and improves visibility through the eye slits in your helm). Keep your lance upright.

At the last possible moment, drop your lance down and slightly to the left side of your horse's neck, so that its point is across the tilt barrier. Cradle the shaft of the lance in the crook of your right arm. Aim for your opponent's chest, which is the

Ride hard along the tilt barrier, leaning forward. Lower your lance across the barrier at the last possible moment.

biggest target and easiest to hit. You may wish to aim for his helm, which requires greater skill and luck and is more likely to cause serious injury or death.

Be prepared for the impact. Whether you hit him or your opponent hits you (or both), there will be a significant shock as the coronal-tipped lance drives home. Upon impact, lean back-

Aim for your opponent's chest, shield, or helm.

ward against the rear wall of your saddle. This lessens the likelihood of being unhorsed.

5. REPEAT AS REQUIRED

Continue to make runs at the other knight until one of the following occurs:

• Your opponent is unseated.
• You have shattered three lances.
• Your opponent is killed or injured beyond his ability to continue.
• Your opponent withdraws (be prepared to accept graciously his humiliation in this case).

If you succeed in unseating your opponent, he will forfeit his horse and armor, unless he is capable of continuing to fight on foot with sword and shield. This is not a recommended practice, but it may happen. If it does, ride at your opponent as you would in the joust. Do not trample the knight unless the joust is being conducted during a state of war between his faction and yours.

PUT OUT AN OIL-WELL FIRE

What You Will Need

- One Athey wagon—a robotically controlled vehicle with a ladder boom, designed to hold explosives in the oil stream
- 200 pounds of 80 percent dynamite
- Multiple high-pressure water hoses
- 8,000–16,000 gallon-per-minute water pumps and adequate water supply—fresh or salt, though fresh is preferred if the fire is on land.
- Two pairs of cotton coveralls
- One balaclava
- Earplugs
- Burn ointment
- Soap, water, and a towel

 Time Required

Three or four days, depending on cleanup of the wellhead.

Background

Oil-well fires are one of the hazards of the petroleum industry. Land- and sea-based wells are at risk of explosion from a number of sources, and great caution is taken to avoid them. When a wellhead catches fire, it is very dangerous, causes significant environmental damage, and represents a severe economic toll.

Instructions

1. TAKE THE EASY WAY OUT

An oil-well fire is big, loud, and scary, but it's still just a fire. And as with any fire, there are a few essential rules:

• It needs fuel to keep burning.
• It needs to stay hot enough to burn.
• It must have a source of oxygen.

Do not fall into the trap of using photogenic contraptions such as jet engines mounted on a tank chassis—this looks good but is cumbersome and of questionable efficiency—or going right for the fire's throat with an explosive charge. Try the simple solutions first.

First, is it possible to turn the oil off? If the control valve wasn't destroyed in the initial blast or burned out by the fire, lay a mist of water on the wellhead for protection and approach on foot to close the valve.

If the valve has been destroyed, connect your pumps to a large water source and begin hosing the fire down. Ninety percent of the oil fires in Kuwait were hosed out of existence this way. The water will cool the oil down below its ignition point and push the oil stream away from the fire. Between dropping the temperature and separating flame from fuel, the fire will go out.

If these solutions work, instruction 3 will no longer be required. Proceed to 2, 4, and 5.

2. CLEAN AND STRAIGHTEN

The area around the wellhead will be a large mess. If the explosion that initiated the fire was large enough, it will have caused piping, rigging, and other material to drop around the head and make access and repair difficult. If the fire is intense enough, it may have melted the valve, assuming it wasn't destroyed in the blast. To further complicate things, as the oil has burned, it will have covered the wellhead with a thick coating of black grunge, sometimes called coke. Finally, the blast may have bent the pipe in such a way that the oil is not moving vertically.

You must correct all of these conditions.

Clear the mess from the wellhead. Pull larger items of loose debris away with cables and heavy equipment, but for the detail work, especially clearing the oil grunge off the piping, get in close. Put on two pairs of cotton coveralls (cotton will not burn or melt as many synthetics do) and a balaclava. Eye protection in the form of goggles is recommended. Approach the wellhead while a fire hose is sprayed on you. Make sure you are not hit with the full force or a stream of the water. This is the dirtiest and most frightening part of the job, but the method is safe and works well.

Approach the fire wearing two pairs of cotton overalls and a balaclava.
Have your crew maintain a mist of water on your back to
protect you from burns.

IMPORTANT NOTE

If you have succeeded in blowing the fire out with a water mist as described in instruction 1 above, continuing to spray the area with water is advised to reduce the chance of accidentally reigniting the fire.

Clear the grunge using hand tools and remove any remaining wreckage. This may be enough to straighten the flow. If not, you'll have to cut the bent section of pipe out. Use a high-pressure water cutter. Do not use saws or other items likely to cause a spark.

If the oil flow is going straight up and the wellhead has been cleaned enough to accept a new valve, this step is completed.

3. RIG EXPLOSIVES

In spite of what people say to the contrary, when you use explosives to extinguish an oil fire, you aren't consuming all the oxygen around it. What you're really doing is using a sudden, sharp blast to separate the fire from the oil. The explosion cuts the link between the well and the flame above it, and the fire goes out.

It is the same concept as blowing out birthday candles. A large enough puff of wind applied in the right place will extinguish almost any fire.

Rig 200 pounds of 80 percent dynamite (a specialized type of dynamite with about 80 percent of the strength per pound of standard TNT) on the boom end of your Athey wagon, and move the explosives package into the oil stream, above the well-head. Run your water hoses on it at the same time, as the stream of water will cool things down and help the separation of oil and fire.

Detonate the explosives. After the blast, the fire will be out.

4. CAP OFF

Clean up any remaining burrs or edges on the pipe end and install a new control valve. The valve should be in the open position until it is firmly installed to avoid the pressure of the oil blowing it off the pipe end. Use non-sparking tools while working on the valve. Once it's bolted in place and secure, close the new valve.

5. CLEAN UP

Shower, using plenty of pumice soap. Treat any burns with ointment, unless they are second-degree or worse, in which case, see a doctor.

RAPPEL OFF THE
EIFFEL TOWER

What You Will Need

• Two 300-meter lengths of Kernmantle rope, 11 millimeters (mm) in diameter. A dynamic rope is recommended to allow some stretch and avoid shocking the rope when it's under a load.

• A heavy-duty climbing harness with dual points of connection (also known as a seat harness)

• A Guide-Rappel-Backup (GRB)—your safety device, made from a four-foot loop of 5-mm Kernmantle rope

• One dozen locking steel carabiners

• "Ice-cube" trays—a low-friction plastic guide that protects your rope as it passes over sharp edges

• Canvas padding

• A climbing helmet with chin strap

• Sunglasses

• Leather or Kevlar gloves—to prevent rope burns on fingers

• A five-bar aluminum rappel rack—a device for creat-

ing friction on a rope as you rappel, by threading the
rope between metal bars held in a frame
• Multiple, nondescript backpacks of the variety used
by low-budget travelers
• Multiple, nondescript, low-budget-looking friends to
haul the backpacks (four minimum)
• Round-trip plane tickets to Paris

⏰ Time Required

Allow one hour for ascent, thirty minutes for setup, and about
ten minutes for the descent.

☞ Background

The Eiffel tower is approximately 324 meters tall, though the
upper platform (where you will rappel from) is at 276 meters.
From the second deck to the top is a relatively straight drop, but
from there down the tower's four legs flare out dramatically. In
some respects, this will make the rappel easier than a straight drop.

Before you start, it is recommended that you reconnoiter
the Tower, particularly the upper platform. You'll need a good,
solid structural element, such as a beam or girder, to secure
your rope to, and it is advisable to have this and the setup clear
in your mind before you arrive for the real thing.

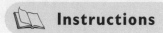 **Instructions**

1. GETTING THERE

Get to the top of the Tower. This can prove tricky, as the staff may wonder why you are hauling climbing gear to the top with you. It is strongly recommended that you manage this by dividing the gear up among two to four friends, who will congregate at the upper platform in ones or twos. Make sure they blend in with the rest of the crowd. Unless you have very good wind and strong legs, use the elevators. There are 1,792 steps to the top.

Be sure you are wearing your harness and have most of your personal gear handy and set up before you get to the Tower. This will save time. Conceal the harness under a baggy coat or untucked shirt.

2. CREATE A DISTRACTION

Before you start setting up the rope, get one or more of your accomplices to stage a loud, raucous, and highly distracting diversion. Fainting or a seizure will work well, as long as they keep attention away from you for at least 15 minutes.

All but one of your remaining assistants will be charged with standing between you and the Tower staff, to obscure the view of you as you set up.

3. SECURE THE LINE

The remaining member of your team will help you get set up, in particular to secure the rappeling line to a structural element. Wrap the beam with the canvas padding to prevent the rope from being damaged or cut by corners or sharp edges. Even a relatively dull edge can damage the rope.

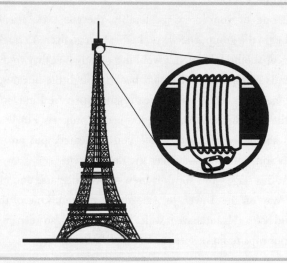

Secure your rappel line to a structural member at the upper platform with a tension anchor. Be sure to pad the member with canvas.

At the railing edge, secure the ice-cube trays where the ropes will pass over the railing. They can be tied off, allowing for some stretch in the ropes holding them in place. Secure the primary rappel line and the safety line to two parts of the structure, using a tension anchor.

4. ON ROPE

Connect your rappel rack to the rope, and your GRB to the rope below the rappel rack.

5. SAFETY CHECK

Have one of your crew, preferably the most experienced climber in the group, check you before you go over. All buckles and gear should be "safed": webbing on any belt that your life depends on should be doubled back through the buckles; all carabiners checked to make sure the gates are closed and *locked;* and the rack checked to be sure it is set up properly. Finally, the GRB should be checked. Once you're cleared, put on your gloves and work your way over the railing edge.

At this stage, your support crew should disperse and make their way off the Tower, to wait at the bottom. One of them should hail a cab and have it wait. They should also keep an eye on your rope to make sure no one interferes with it.

6. DOWN

Lower yourself down the rope, keeping your feet in front of you, spread to the same width as your shoulders. Resist the urge to jump and drop. This is only done in action films, and it isn't the proper, safe approach to rappeling. "Walk" your way down the tower, changing pressure on the bars on the rack as you go. If the going seems too stiff, drop one bar out of the rack.

With luck, no one will notice you until it is too late. You're counting on the element of surprise as your ally, but don't dillydally to take in the view or chat with tourists as you pass the lower observation decks.

7. OFF ROPE

When you hit the bottom, get off the rope as quickly as possible. You're going to abandon the ropes and gear on the Tower as part of the price of the experience, jump in the cab, and head for the airport.

SINK A SUBMARINE

What You Will Need

• One Oliver Hazard Perry–class (FFG-7) antisubmarine frigate or one Arleigh Burke–class destroyer—arrange for use through the U.S. Department of Defense.
• Command rank in the U.S. Navy or Naval Reserve
• One or two SH-60F Seahawk Light Airborne Multi-Purpose System (LAMPS) helicopters with dipping sonar
• One P-3C III Orion aircraft
• Antisubmarine Rocket (ASROC) equipped with Mark 46 torpedo warheads
• Sonar buoys
• A bunch of friends

 Time Required

Allow two to three hours.

☞ Background

Antisubmarine Warfare (ASW) is one of the most difficult and complex areas of naval combat. During World War I, the first attempts to combat the predations of submarines attacking supply convoys to Europe were largely unsuccessful. Things improved markedly during the Second World War, though early on in the conflict the submarines held a distinct advantage because of limited availability of underwater detection equipment for the ASW vessels. By the end of the war, the tide had turned and submarines were at great risk. Scientists developed more effective systems for tracking submarines, and the weapons used against them improved dramatically. As a result, German U-boat crews had the highest casualty rates by percentages of any arm of the German military, a reflection of the ability of ASW forces to find and sink the subs and the fact that when a sub sinks, there is little chance of escape.

In response to the crippling casualties inflicted on commercial shipping and naval forces during the war and the rise of the submarine as one of the most dangerous weapons of the Cold War, antisubmarine warfare has risen to a high art, led by advances in underwater acoustical detection systems, most commonly known as SONAR (for Sound Navigation and Ranging), though there are technologies in development that use very refined lasers to generate images in the water. At this time, SONAR is still the most common detection device, though it has been dramatically improved since its invention nearly a century ago. Combined with "smart" weapons capable of independently seeking out targets, modern ship design, and years of practice and refinement, ASW is not only a high art, but a deadly one as well.

ASW is carried out by fast-attack submarines, which are equally effective against surface vessels and other submarines, but for this scenario a more traditional approach, using a destroyer or frigate, is suggested—though in concert with airborne sub detection systems.

 Instructions

1. GATHER YOUR TEAM AND CONFIRM YOUR ORDERS

According to a source at the Pentagon, the critical element in ASW is that it is a "team sport." For this reason you'll need several friends to help you.

Your team will need to include a qualified crew for your frigate or destroyer, as well as aircrews for the Seahawks and Orion. Once you have them on board their respective vehicles, transit to your target area to search for the sub.

It is necessary to be sure a state of war exists between you and the nation owning the submarine you are going to sink. Alternatively, make sure you have permission to attack any unidentified subs in your area. Failure to meet either of these requirements can result in court martial, loss of benefits, and jail time.

2. FIND A SUB

Before you sink a submarine, you have to find it. In the modern age, this is no mean feat. The newest generation of submarines is so quiet the subs create a "hole" in the background noise of the ocean. However, this can also give them away. With natural and man-made sounds constantly being produced in the oceans, the seas are an intensely noisy place. Since a sub is so quiet and the sea is so noisy, you can even find one by looking for an area indicating intense silence on your sonar display.

If a submarine is suspected of operating in your area, begin by deploying the LAMPS helicopter(s) and the P-3C Orion aircraft. These should begin a search pattern with passive sonar, either dipping the sonar in at specific points (from the Seahawks) or dropping floating sonar buoys (from the Orion) in a set pattern. As an aircraft picks up information, the data will be transmitted by encrypted radio back to the Combat Information Center (CIC) on your ship, where your tactical officer can assess it and coordinate the attack.

This assumes you are using passive listening techniques—using acoustical sensors to watch for noises that may be a sub. When a fast-attack sub, such as the American Los Angeles–class or the Russian Alpha, is tracking an enemy sub, it is usually done with passive sonar—by listening for noises (or the lack of noises) that the target makes. Alternatively, one may use *active* sonar, which means sending out sound waves in the water and listening to see if they reflect off anything. This is more direct and fairly effective, but it has the negative effect of alerting your prey to your own location. Active sonar is most commonly used when in attack mode rather than in search mode.

3. IDENTIFY YOUR TARGET

Compare the sound "footprint" of the target sub against recordings of known submarines and classes of submarines. Over the years, navy ships, submarines, and planes (as well as other intelligence sources) have provided a library of footprints for allied and enemy submarines, accurate enough to identify particular boats. By contrasting the sound of the sub you are tracking to this library, you will know what you're up against as you approach it and help to confirm that you are not attacking a friendly vessel.

4. GIVE CHASE

Route your ship toward the target, switching to active sonar as necessary to confirm the location and lock the coordinates into the attack computers on your weapons systems.

Once your attack is underway, the sub has several options. For starters, it may change depths and its heading relative to you. Differences in water temperature and density can serve to deflect sonar. If the sub turns end on to you (bow or stern first, rather than broadside), it presents a much smaller cross section relative to the sonar wave, making it more difficult to track and target. The sub will also operate at lower speeds or even stop its engines to keep noise to a minimum.

5. FIRE TORPEDO(ES)

Initiate your attack with an ASROC, a vertically launched missile. Program the attack coordinates into the ASROC firing systems and launch the first missile. Its rocket motor will carry the warhead to the general area of the sub, lowering it into the sea gently on a parachute. Once in the water, the parachute detaches and the ASROC deploys its weapon, a Mark 46 torpedo.

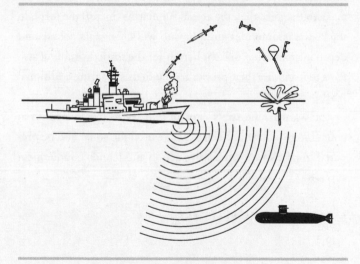

Once you have acquired the submarine, program the coordinates into the ASROC, and fire the weapon. The ASROC will lower into the water by parachute, detach itself from the parachute, and track the sub.

The Mark 46 torpedo uses active sonar to target the sub. Once it has a fix, it will actively pursue its target at high speed, turning to follow the sub. If possible, it will sink the sub by detonating directly against the boat's hull, in which case a breach of the hull will cause flooding and serious damage, if not out-and-out sinking. Failing this, a detonation in close proximity to the sub may cause an overpressure situation, damaging the sub or splitting the pressure hull and flooding the submarine. In this case, multiple torpedoes may be required.

Once the torpedo has locked onto the sub, evasive action at high speed is to be expected. The sub will also launch countermeasures, i.e., noisemakers that mimic the sound of the sub and make more noise than the actual submarine does. If the torpedo tracks the countermeasure, the sub will change its course and depth in an effort to make it harder for the torpedo guiding systems to reacquire their proper target. In this case, fire additional ASROCs.

Be warned, the sub's captain will try to fire torpedoes at your ship to sink you. Keep a close ear on the sonar and be prepared to take your own evasive action and launch countermeasures.

6. REPEAT 2–5 AS NECESSARY

CHOP DOWN A 200-FOOT SEQUOIA

What You Will Need

- Several two-man crosscut saws of varying lengths—several Canadian and U.S. firms still make these; try the Internet for dealers.
- Axes, well sharpened—get these from a lumberjack supply company.
- Twenty springboards—you can make these or buy them from an antique dealer.
- Kerosene or a similar solvent
- One giant sequoia
- Two six-inch steel pins
- Two 40-foot lengths of ½-inch rope
- Leather gloves
- Hard hats
- Eye protection (goggles or approved safety glasses)
- Water
- One very strong friend, with an emphasis on upper body strength

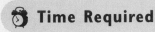 **Time Required**

Allow three to five days.

Background

The giant sequoias are among the largest and most impressive living organisms on the planet. No land- or sea-dwelling animal alive today is even close to the size of this tree. Though there is one variety of tree that gets larger in diameter, and three species that get taller, none of them combine height and girth to match the sequoia. The largest-known tree in the species, the General Sherman, as it has been nicknamed, is estimated to weigh 2,500 metric tons, is about 275 feet tall, and is over 102 feet in circumference at its base. The bark layer alone may be two feet thick. Sequoias are constantly growing, adding as much wood as is found in a 60-foot fir tree every year. They are also hardy, naturally resistant to rot and decay. Sawdust piles may still be found from the cutting of the trees 100 years ago.

The sequoias are a relatively picky tree, with a range limited to the western slopes of the Sierra Nevada, typically at altitudes between 5,000 and 7,000 feet above sea level. Furthermore, the majority of them are found on federal land, where they are a protected species. This complicates our scenario, requiring you to find one of the few remaining on private land and negotiating its purchase before you cut it down. Attempting to cut one of the trees on federal land will result in jail time.

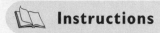 **Instructions**

1. ASSESS THE SITUATION

Once you have found a tree that you can purchase, negotiate the price. Expect to pay up to $100,000. Get a contract executed and be sure you have legal right to the tree and are not liable for any damage to surrounding trees or structures.

Once you have this in hand, it is time to assess the situation and plan the cut. Toppling a sequoia is a major undertaking, not a simple exercise in backyard brush clearing.

Given the size and weight of a sequoia, planning the cut and the fall is essential. Take a look at the tree from all angles, taking into account any natural lean it has, as well as the wind conditions during the cutting. Windy conditions over five knots, especially if the sequoia is not surrounded by other trees or sheltered by the terrain, will make the cutting unpredictable and dangerous. Check with the local meteorologist and look for a period of three to five days with little or no wind.

Walk the areas around the tree, looking for where you can drop it without damaging the tree itself or adjacent ones, and bear in mind that you'll need access to it once it's down.

2. BUILD A PLATFORM

You don't cut trees this sturdy at the base. You will need to go up the trunk about 15 feet in order to be able to deal with the tree's girth. This is done with springboards (long, wooden boards wide enough and strong enough for a person to work from, with steel tips to bite into the wood of the tree) and axes. You will make small notches in the bark with an ax and insert a springboard into them, using each one as a working platform to get to the next elevation. Eventually, you'll reach your chosen cutting height, at which point you'll need to put in several

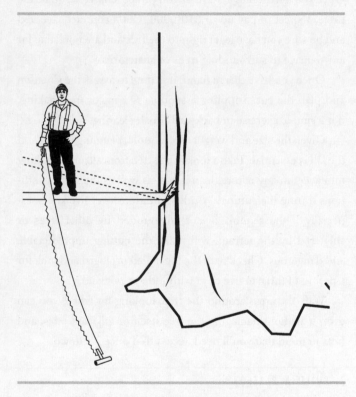

Cut a notch into the side of the tree, using your ax.
Set a springboard into the notch as a work platform. From each platform
location, cut another notch higher up and set a new platform in that
notch until you reach the height you will cut from.

springboards to develop a broader, more comfortable platform to work from.

Your friend should be doing the same thing on the opposite side of the tree from you.

Rig two ropes on opposite sides of the tree where you and your partner will stand. These should be tied off to steel pegs driven into the bark below your cut line.

3. CUT A NOTCH

Once you are at the correct height, use axes to begin cutting a notch in the tree on the same side as the direction you want to drop the tree. The notch should extend into the tree approximately one-quarter to one-third of the tree's diameter. Cut too far and the tree may fall prematurely, which will cause splintering and damage to the trunk on the side opposite and reduce the saleable wood.

Once the notch has been cut, establish the springboard platform on the opposite side of the tree from the notch. NEVER try to use the crosscut in the large notch, as the tree will pinch the blade as you cut. Cut a second, smaller notch as a starting point for your saw, and begin cutting. You may use a "beavertail" (a one-man saw with a blunt end opposite the handle) initially, while the width of the wood you are cutting is still small. You should trade off cutting at this time with your friend.

Once the wood depth being cut exceeds ten feet, you will need to use a two-man saw. Start with a shorter saw, about 15 feet, to allow for the wood and the length of saw exposed at either end as you pull. As you get deeper into the tree, the wood diameter will increase up to 35 feet, which means very heavy work in moving the saw. You may counter this by continuing with a smaller two-man saw, angling the saw across the tree, moving to the left of your original cut and cutting there for an hour; then move to the right of the original cut and do the same there for an hour. Use the larger saws once you have completed cutting as much as possible with the shorter saws.

As you cut into the trunk, pause periodically to squirt kerosene on the blade. This will help dissolve any sap that accumulates and keep the saw blade from gumming up.

Remember, you will be working from the springboard platforms. Watch your step.

4. KEEP SAWING

As you approach the center of the trunk, the weight of the tree will begin to pull it toward the large notch. Keep cutting until a noticeable gap, 12 to 15 inches, begins to open. Judgment is called for here: if the gap is opening slowly, you may continue cutting; if the gap opens abruptly, it is time to get off the springboard. We recommend practice on smaller trees to gain experience in judging this.

5. JUMP

Because of the size of a giant sequoia, when the tree is ready to go over it will tilt toward the first notch steadily. At this point get off the platform to avoid being hit by the trunk if it slips sideways or backward. Do not leave the platform with the saw in your hands or near your person. Use the ropes you rigged before starting to lower yourself down the trunk, and then move away from the trunk. If the tree starts to go quickly, jump, aiming for the pile of wood chips and sawdust that will have accumulated at the base of the tree.

6. CLEAN THE LOG

Once the tree has fallen, trim and remove its branches and top, which have little value. Cut the trunk into manageable sections using the crosscut saw and load them on trucks for delivery to the mill.

SMUGGLE TOP-SECRET DOCUMENTS

What You Will Need

- One or more top-secret documents
- Two Boy Scouts, one from each side of the U.S.-Canadian border
- One accomplice from across the border
- One long-shank ⅛-inch drill bit mounted in a drill press
- An ice pick or 12-inch piece of stiff wire (#14 AWG—American Wire Gauge, the standard for wire measurement)
- An invitation to a Boy Scout event at a controlled border
- One small Canadian flag
- A camera
- One reversible windbreaker
- Latex gloves
- Lightweight gloves
- One Seattle Mariners cap

- One Toronto Argonauts cap
- Two bandanas, one red, one blue

Time Required

One hour prep, one to two hours hanging around, looking like you belong time, 30 seconds for exchange.

Background

The Boy Scouts, American and otherwise, have a long tradition of encouraging cooperation and understanding. Historically, they have been sponsors of international events that bring diverse scout troops from around the world together in an unfettered environment.

Every spring, the Boy Scouts of America and Canada (along with Girl Scouts, Cub Scouts, Sea Scouts, Blue Birds, Brownies, etc.) gather at the International Border crossing between White Rock, British Columbia, and Blaine, Washington. Between 4,000 and 6,000 scouts and family members show up, and the border is closed to vehicle traffic while the scouts march across to signify unity and international goodwill. There is minimal monitoring and no hassles by the border patrol. During the crossing, it is customary for American and Canadian scouts to exchange national flags.

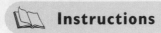 **Instructions**

1. REDUCE AND STORE THE DOCUMENT

Use a commercial copier to reduce the original document to one-quarter of its original size. It is essential to have the minimum amount of paper. Otherwise, the document will not roll up tightly enough.

Procure one small Canadian flag, mounted to a ¼-inch diameter dowel approximately nine inches long. Mount the shaft in the drill press, with the flag end down and the butt-end of the shaft straight up under the drill. Drill eight inches into the shaft. Clear excess sawdust from the hole, and insert the reduced document, using an ice pick or stiff wire to slide it in as far as possible.

Fill the open end of the hole with a mixture of sawdust and wood glue. Immediately invert the flag so the plugged end is down. Allow to dry, then sand any excess glue or wood away.

It is critical that you wear latex gloves during the handling of the flags, documents, and other items to avoid leaving fingerprints. When you handle the flag at the exchange point, be sure to wear your light gloves for the same reason. The weather in the spring is cool, fortunately, making the gloves seem appropriate.

2. BLEND IN

Get to the Canadian side of the border by 10:00 A.M. The crossing starts at about 1:00 P.M., but the parking is difficult as the morning wears on, and having quick access to your car is important.

Spend some time wandering around with the crowd. The primary activities before the march are buying and trading badges and scouting paraphernalia, talking to people, and enjoying the day. It is essential you take part in this. If you don't or appear nervous, you won't fit into the crowd, and there are border agents, Canadian Mounties, and Washington State Patrol representatives around. Do not catch their attention.

Sign in at the Canadian registration table (located in the activities building on the west side of the park on the Canadian side). Give them a false name and a number from an Eastern Canadian troop. They will not ask for identification. They will give you some of the small Canadian flags. You'll substitute your prepared flag for one of the genuine ones.

You should come to the event wearing the reversible windbreaker (with different colors inside than out) and a long-sleeved shirt over a T-shirt. Put on the Argonauts cap.

3. SPOT THE HANDOFF

At about 12:30 P.M., the scouts will form up in columns on opposite sides of the border. Take the red bandana and wear it around your neck, pointed end back. This is the recognition sign to your contact. He or she will be wearing the blue bandana in the same way.

At 1:00 P.M., the columns will begin to march across the border and through the Peace Arch that marks the crossing.

Do not give the prepared flag to your scout until you have spotted your contact.

4. MAKE THE PASS

Your contact will have entered the column on the U.S. side as close to the end of the line as possible. Once you are through the Peace Arch, stop and begin taking pictures of the scene, the participants, etc. This gives you a perfect opportunity to scrutinize the American column.

When you spot your handoff, make eye contact and proceed to march in parallel with your scout to the American side. Your contact should hand an American flag to his scout. Do the same, giving your scout the prepared Canadian flag. You and

Drill out the staff of the flag and insert the secret documents, plugging the hole with glue and sawdust. The scouts will swap flags at the border crossing.

your contact should point out the other's scout to your own and encourage them to swap flags.

5. LOOK NONCHALANT

Once the handoff has been made, you are free and clear. Blend into the crowd, join in the singing, listen to the music, and then quietly excuse yourself and your scout—a quick trip to the men's room is adequate if anyone is paying attention. Once you get to the rest area, step into the facility, wash your hands, observing who enters after you. If they don't appear threatening, retrieve your car and leave the area. If you have reason to believe you are being followed, return to the crowd and mix in. As you do so, remove your windbreaker and take off the long-sleeved shirt. Casually turn the windbreaker inside out, revealing a different color, and put it on. Swap the Argonauts cap for the Mariners cap.

Stay in the crowd, then move with them toward the parking area once enough of them start to leave.

SWIM THROUGH THE BYPASS TUNNELS AT HOOVER DAM

What You Will Need

- One caving helmet with chin strap—do not use a helmet with a faceshield as it will impede your ability to get to your emergency air supply.
- Titanium-impregnated 9-millimeter (mm) neoprene wet suit and gloves—available from most scuba-diving suppliers and whitewater-rafting outfitters
- Knee and elbow pads
- Face mask (scuba-style, covering eyes and nose only)
- One emergency air supply, a.k.a. a pony bottle (small-scale pressurized air bottle with built-in mouthpiece) attached to your life vest—it must be placed high enough on the vest to be easily accessible at a moment's notice.
- 600 feet of 11-mm rope and a rappeling rig (See Rappel Off the Eiffel Tower, p. 86, for additional information.)
- One self-inflating Mae West–style life vest—if you

can't get one in your local sporting-goods or boaters-supply store, look under the seat of a commercial airliner.

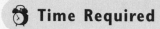 Time Required

Allow 30 to 40 minutes to set up, and approximately 30 to 60 seconds to make the run.

Background

Hoover Dam is located about 30 minutes' drive from Las Vegas. Built in 1934 to harness the power of the Colorado River, it was once the largest and most powerful dam in the world. This is no longer true, but Hoover (originally known as Boulder Dam) is still an impressive structure. From the top of the dam to the base is a drop of 727 feet.

On the upstream side of the Dam sits Lake Mead. On this side, to the left and right of the Dam, are two spillways, referred to as the Arizona and Nevada spillways respectively. The flow of water through them is controlled by eight drum gates, four on each spillway. The gates are lowered or raised to drain off excess water in the lake or to meet water commitments downstream.

Each spillway connects to a 50-foot diameter tunnel that drops at a sharp angle to intercept the old bypass lines that were used to divert water around the dam construction site in the 1930s. The upriver half of the old tunnels were plugged long ago, but the lower halves were reused to connect to the spillways. They empty out downstream from the power plant.

IMPORTANT NOTE

Do not access the Dam through any of the four intake towers in Lake Mead. They are protected by debris screens and feed the turbines in the powerhouse. Trying to run through that way would result in death.

 Instructions

1. ADD WATER

The only practical way to ride Hoover Dam is through the bypass tunnels. To do this, there must be adequate water flowing through them. There are two ways you can manage this. First, wait to run when the waters in Lake Mead are high enough to flow into the spillways. You could stop by and check regularly, but the best way to gauge this is to call the Dam's public information officer and tell them you are a photographer looking for an opportunity to photograph the spillways in action. Ask them to call you and let you know when the time is right. You can also wait for a good rainy period.

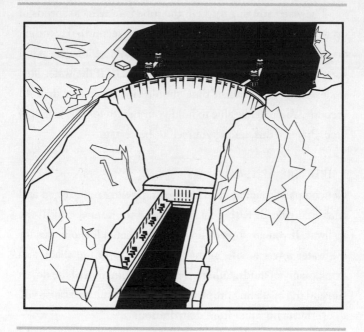

Go to the Arizona spillway on the eastern side of the dam.

If you are not patient or are in a period of dry weather or the Dam's public information officer is not cooperative, have the drum gates on the Arizona spillway opened so that the spillway is running at close to maximum capacity. The easiest way to manage this is to bribe the valve operator.

At the downstream end of the spillway, right before it hits the tunnel, there is a 36-foot-deep pool. This is here to improve the hydrodynamics of the water run, and you must be able to get clear of it. An inadequate water flow will make this impossible.

The water running through the tube is moving at speeds of up to 120 miles per hour (or 176 feet per second), depending on the volume of water. The tunnel is 2,200 feet long, so at full speed you will pass through in 12.5 seconds. If the water flow is slower, the total transit time should not be greater than 40 seconds. You must be able to hold your breath for this length of time. Practice this, timing yourself to be certain.

2. INTO THE SPILLWAY

Get completely suited up with your rappeling rope rigged and anchored to a BFR (big fat rock) near the tunnel end of the spillway. If you are forced to wait more than a few minutes for the water levels to rise in the spillway, stay in the shade and drink plenty of fluids. Otherwise, the combination of the desert sun and the insulating properties of your wet suit will cause you to overheat and suffer from dehydration.

Once there is adequate water flow into the spillway, drop the loose end of your rope over the edge of the spillway, remembering to pad the point where the rope will rub against the concrete lip.

IMPORTANT NOTE

Do not *under any circumstances* try and go over the drum gates into the spillway from the lake side. The fall and tumbling will kill or seriously injure you.

Rappel down the rope and enter the water in the spillway.

IMPORTANT NOTE

Be sure you are completely ready to go before you start down the rope. All your gear should be on and in proper working order. You'll have no time for adjustments once you get into the spillway.

3. FEET FORWARD

As you move down the spillway, orient yourself so you are faceup, lying as straight as possible, with your arms at your side and feet forward. If you enter the tunnel sideways or at a sharp angle, you will present more of a profile to the water and be more apt to tumble and be pulled into the walls of the tunnel. If you tumble, you will be seriously injured or killed, and you will not be able to recover easily from a tumble once you start.

4. BREATHE DEEPLY

Take several deep breaths before you enter the tunnel, and hold your last one before you do. If you do get into a slower flow, use the pony bottle to supplement your air supply.

5. SPLASHDOWN

The tube will spit you out into the Colorado below the Dam and (more important) below the power plant and its bone-crunching turbines. Pull the emergency inflate-handles on your life jacket and begin to make your way to the beach.

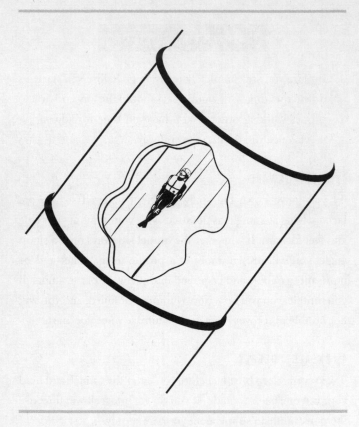

As you transit the bypass tunnel, keep your feet in front of you and your body straight—to avoid tumbling.

GUIDE AND SURFACE A NUCLEAR SUB THROUGH THE ICE

What You Will Need

• One used SSN-637 Sturgeon-class nuclear attack sub, or one SSN-688 or 688i Los Angeles-class nuclear attack sub, with crew

• Nuclear fuel—states from the former Soviet Union are the best place to start.

• BQQ-10 sonar system with experienced operator

• Long johns, winter pants, sweater, gloves, and a warm coat

• U.S. army–issue winter overboots

• Snow goggles

• Binoculars

• Rifle with sniper scope and ammunition

• Flag—U.S. or any nation of your choice—you can use your own from Form an Independent Nation, p. 128, if you've already formed one.

⏰ Time Required

Allow five to six weeks for transit to the North Pole and back to open water.

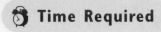 **Background**

The idea of operating a nuclear submarine under an ice pack originated during the early years of the Cold War, when both American and Russian military planners decided to experiment with the idea of hiding ballistic-missile submarines under the Arctic ice, where they would be closer to their targets and hidden from detection by attack submarines looking for them. In order to make this idea work, it became necessary to learn how to surface through the ice to fire the missiles.

To begin this project, you must acquire the use of an appropriate submarine. Older Russian Whiskey-class diesel boats are advertised on the World Wide Web, but do not let the seemingly cheap prices (under U.S. $500,000) tempt you. The air-breathing nature of diesel-powered submarines makes them impractical—the engines must be run at regular intervals to recharge the batteries used to power the maneuvering motors while submerged. This requires the submarine to either surface for lengthy periods or to operate a snorkel that expels exhaust and takes in fresh air from the surface. Access to open water or areas of thin ice (polyanas) that the sub can penetrate is unpredictable, making the diesel approach unworkable and impractical.

Nuclear submarines, by contrast, are not hampered by this limitation, using a contained nuclear reactor to provide propulsion. They are also capable of manufacturing air and drinking water and may remain submerged as long as food supplies last. A nuclear sub, then, is the only choice for a submerged trip to the North Pole.

The SSN-637 series of attack boats had a successful record of traversing the ice pack on many missions, including surfacing at the pole, as have the SSN-688s and newer 688is. The techniques for navigating in confined spaces were developed into a fine art on these submarines. Navy documents indicate that there are several still intact but unused:

SSN 653 Ray
SSN 660 Sandlance
SSN 675 Bluefish
SSN 679 Silverside
SSN 680 Redfish a.k.a. William H. Bates
SSN 681 Batfish
SSN 683 Parche (At this writing, the Parche is the
    only active boat in the class, but will be decommis-
    sioned soon.)
SSN 686 L. Mendal Rivers
SSN 687 Richard B. Russell

You may wish to examine the possibilities of using one of the modern SSN-688 and 688i Los Angeles–class attack subs, but they are in active use by the U.S. Navy and unlikely to be available.

Instructions

I. GETTING THERE

Once your sub is fully provisioned and ready to go, head north through the Bering Sea toward the Bering Strait. Summer months are easiest in terms of having the least amount of ice to transit, though winter transits are possible. The ice pack is the limiting factor. The further south it extends, the longer you'll need to be submerged.

2. SUBMERGE

During the summer months, you will have a long, clear cruise through the Bering and into the Chukchi Sea before you hit the permanent ice pack, which will make safe passage and navigation much easier. The average depth of the Chukchi is only 253 feet, and much of it is shallower. If you transit this area during the winter months, when the ice pack has reached its southern-most extent, you will encounter ice ridges or "keels" extending down from the surface as deep as 195 feet. These will reduce your ability to maneuver.

Travel north, following a bearing to intercept the Pole. When you sight the ice pack, prepare to submerge.

Prior to submerging, communicate your position by radio to the U.S. Coast Guard. Double-check your location and bearing. It is absolutely essential that you take great care in your navigation from here on out if you are using a 637-class sub. Its gimbel-type gyroscopic navigation systems don't work as well as you approach the North Pole because the rotational speed of the earth in the higher latitudes affects their accuracy—it tends to push the gyro over on its side, impairing function. Once under the ice, you will not have the luxury of the constant position checks Global Positioning System (GPS) satellites give to surface vessels. You can check periodically, but only when you surface. If you've got an L.A.-class sub, you use an electronic static gyro navigation system or a ring laser gyro, both of which have little difficulty in dealing with the high latitudes.

You also have the benefit of a different technique for navigation at the Pole, developed by the navy. Once you get close enough to the Pole, around 84 to 85 degrees north latitude, the functionality of longitude and latitude lines becomes problematic. While the physical separation between latitude lines does not change, longitude lines get closer and closer together.

To combat this, switch your navigation system over to polar mode. In effect, navigation is performed as though the Pole had been moved to the middle of the Pacific Ocean on the equator. This squares up the navigation system and reduces the margin of error.

Surface through polyanas periodically to check your position against GPS satellite fixes. Using newer navigation systems, a sub can travel as much as two weeks between fixes and still be very confident of its location (within 2,500 feet).

Another trick to under-ice navigation is to check the bottom depth and contours against those known for the area you believe you are in. An unusually deep bottom when you think you are in a shallow area is a dead giveaway that you've taken a wrong turn.

Once prepared, close all watertight doors and openings into the sub, making sure you have a "green" board (indicating the boat is ready to submerge). Deploy the bow planes for maneuvering.

Submerge.

3. VIGILANCE

As you transit under the ice in the Bering or Chukchi Sea, proceed slowly, at five to seven knots. The BQQ-10 sonar now available will monitor the bottom depth below your keel, the distance to the ice above you, and the depth of ice coming your way, giving you plenty of warning. However, you must have adequate time to react to any hazards, and a lower speed is the best approach.

If the sonar detects an ice ridge in your path, there are a couple of tricks to avoiding it. First, check for "fade ranging." If a sonar contact of an ice keel disappears when you get within 300 yards of it, you will pass 25 feet below it. This is a function of the geometries of the sonar system and its location on the submarine.

Second, trust in luck and the "narrow sail" theory: the sail on a nuclear sub (the portion that extends up from the main hull) is not wide, measuring eight to nine feet across. If the sonar suggests that there is no ice directly ahead of the sub or within six degrees to either side of the sub, then the sub can pass through the opening with plenty of room to spare.

The rule of travel while you are in the shallow areas is to keep moving straight ahead (to minimize navigational errors) and on course, with your keel 25 feet off the bottom. The sea floor is almost billiard table smooth in the southern approaches to the Arctic Ocean, so bottom features are not the risk, and the closer you are to the bottom, the further you are from the ice.

Keep a constant watch on your ice thickness monitor for polyanas. As the system tracks the ice, normal ice will appear as a ragged line. A polyana will appear as a smooth line. As you pass one, note the start of it on your track. When you pass back to normal ice, note this as the end of the polyana. Perform a Figure 4 turn: execute a 270-degree turn to the starboard, bringing the sub back under the polyana. Take readings of the width of the polyana as you do.

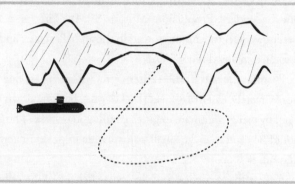

When you pass a polyana, perform a Figure 4 turn, turning the sub through 270 degrees to bring it back under the polyana.

Track the size and location of each polyana you pass, bearing in mind that you can only rely on that location for 30 to 40 minutes (an hour at most), as the ice can move rapidly. Polyanas are your targets for surfacing in an emergency, to conduct on-ice scientific work, or just to check your position. Unfortunately, the only way to find a polyana is to pass underneath it.

4. THE NORTH POLE

When you arrive in the vicinity of the North Pole (the real one, not the magnetic one, which is somewhere under Canada), begin searching for a polyana. Check the ice thickness when you do. Compare the water depth (which includes the ice) to distance from the sub to the bottom of the ice. If the water above is 400 feet, but the distance to the ice is 397, then you've got approximately three feet of ice—well within the capabilities of the 688s and the 637s.

Retrieve the submarine's towed sonar array and deploy your Secondary Propulsion Motor (SPM). This is a 200-horsepower electric motor stowed in the aft ballast tank and can be rotated in any direction.

Position the sub in the center of the polyana at a depth of approximately 150 to 180 feet (keel depth), backing down your speed by using your main engines running in reverse. The SPM should be used to make small adjustments in position and orientation.

Raise your periscope and do a visual check of the polyana, looking for previously undetected ice keels or obstructions. Once completed, lower and secure the periscope and retract the bow planes to avoid damaging them.

For the actual surfacing, you can either go with a "vertical surface" or a "pick-and-blow."

If you go for the vertical surface, start surfacing at 30 feet per minute. At this speed, the sail will punch through the ice and make a crack. Turn on your low-pressure blowers and start filling the main ballast tanks with air. The added buoyancy will bring the sub up.

If you prefer a gentler method, try a pick-and-blow. Gently raise the sub up so that the top of the sail presses to the underside of the ice. Start blowing air into your tanks and let the upward pressure force the sub up through the ice.

Check your GPS location to see how close you are to the Pole. Allow three to ten minutes for the fix to lock in.

Radio in your success.

5. SURFACE HAZARDS

Outside the sub, the conditions are hostile. Air temperatures are exceedingly low. Storms can come up suddenly. The ice can start moving or breaking up. It is not out of the realm of possibility to run into a polar bear on the ice. Polar bears are one of the fiercest predators on earth. When you are at the Pole or anywhere on the ice in the Arctic, you have taken a step down in the food chain from predator to prey.

Before you or anyone else goes out and starts planting flags, take a look around with your binoculars, and always keep a watch posted with an eye toward spotting bear and tracking the whereabouts of any crew you have outside, in case you need to make a hasty departure.

When you've had enough, submerge and head for home, leaving via the Atlantic Ocean. The passage will be easier due to the deeper nature of these waters.

FORM AN INDEPENDENT NATION

What You Will Need

• Land which is either in dispute (a legitimate cultural/historical claim to same is helpful), has never been discovered, or has recently come into existence (the eastern coast of the island of Hawaii, for example).

• A good lawyer with experience in real-estate and international law

• Charisma—remember, you're going to have to talk a lot of people into seeing things your way.

• Hard currency

• One flag

• One constitution

• One national anthem, national bird, national tree, and national flower

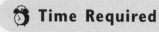 Time Required

Six to twelve months.

☞ Background

History has shown that forming an independent nation is an uphill fight. Very few cases of a group of people creating their own government and country within the confines of a sovereign nation have taken place without bloodshed. The American Revolution, the creation of Israel, and the Palestinian State, the war in the Balkans, and most rebellions against colonial powers have had a high cost in terms of loss of life and damage to or destruction of property.

A strong argument for independent status can be made if the land in question meets two essential criterions: first, no one else already owns it or has a legitimate claim to it; and second, no one else really wants it. If the land you seek to establish dominion over is of strategic, economic, or military value, has huge reserves of natural resources (oil, gold, platinum, fisheries, etc.), or might be a good spot for a nice resort, you're up against a tough battle.

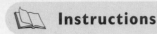 **Instructions**

I. IDENTIFY, ACQUIRE, OCCUPY

There are two possible scenarios to this proposition—buy or incite.

In the first case, buy; with adequate hard currency in hand it is not difficult to approach any of a number of third-world nations and offer to buy some part of their territory outright, along with their recognition of your existence as a sovereign nation. The more cash-starved they are, the higher your chances for success.

Belize (which has several modest islands for sale off the coast), Nicaragua, Fiji, the Philippines, or the Seychelles in the Indian Ocean are good places to start. Contact their departments of state or foreign offices to initiate discussions.

An island can be had for the equivalent of as little as a few tens of thousands to a few millions. Given the likelihood of many low-lying islands being submerged by the effects of global warming on the world's ice caps, many governments may be willing and eager to part with these properties.

When buying the land, set aside an amount of cash for both the purchase price and all fees and deposits required by the local sovereign government. The Seychelles will require, for example, that you deposit two million Seychelles rupees (about U.S. $390,000) in the central bank of Seychelles. In Belize, it is necessary to get a lien landholder's license from the Ministry of Natural Resources. To acquire this license, you must explain how you intend to use the land. (Do not mention publicly your plans to declare independence. This is a private matter between you and high government officials.) In Belize, investors developing land and providing jobs for Belizeans are very welcome. The license, which is just a formality, is usually granted in one to two months. Be warned, any real-estate purchase involving the offshore islands must first be approved by the government *regardless of size,* so make friends in the capital. Other countries have similar requirements.

A variation on this concept is to buy foreign soil of some importance and, after an appropriate waiting period, declare independence from a repressive government. Immediately appeal to the U.S. State Department or the nearest militarily and economically powerful nation for support. Be sure you can demonstrate an active oppression of human rights by your host country. Also, maintain a deep and meaningful relationship with government figures (and their re-election campaigns) from the country you appeal to. Members of parliament, congress, prime ministers, and presidents are all good friends to have in this situation.

For the second option, incite; pick a country with a significant undertone of dissatisfaction on the part of a group who is in the political or cultural minority. Introduce yourselves to this group and provide funding and leadership (this is where charisma is a fundamental requirement) in their drive toward achieving their identity. This has been an established and moderately successful method in Africa, the Balkans, and most colonial states.

This approach is little more than siding with the disenfranchised, raising their awareness and self-confidence, and leading them into a peaceful (if possible) rebellion. Unfortunately, bloodshed is often a result, and as such, this is not a recommended method. Should you feel this is the best approach, contact *Soldier of Fortune* magazine and get references for mercenaries.

Failing either of the two methods described above, you may also try claiming land that is not technically in any jurisdiction or is in dispute. Newly emerging volcanic islands are a good choice, as are parts of Antarctica. Lacking a suitable candidate, you may establish a raised platform in some shallow portion of the ocean and begin creating your own nation by having dirt brought in on barges.

2. FORM A GOVERNMENT

Once you have selected your path to independence, you must start on the road to world recognition.

The first step to legitimacy is to establish a government: you'll need leadership, social servants, and an ironclad constitution. A parliamentary system, coupled with a constitutional monarchy, is recommended. Do not set yourself up as ruler for life. Nothing will bring a peace-keeping force of U.S. Marines into the presidential palace faster than that.

Cover the major issues: human rights, free speech, freedom of religion, free association, etc. Do not miss the lessons learned elsewhere. For example, allowing the citizenry to arm themselves is not a good thing. Poor wording of the constitution leads to unnecessary debate over interpretation and results in a proliferation of attorneys.

IMPORTANT NOTE

Give your country a name. In choosing, go for something simple that rhymes with other common words. This will make composing the lyrics to your national anthem an easier task.

3. APPOINT AMBASSADORS

Appoint friends, businesspeople, and others (either because you owe them favors, think they're capable, or you just want them out of the country) and send them off to be your ambas-

Appoint ambassadors to foreign nations, selecting friends, cronies, and people you want out of the country.

sadors to the major powers. Don't miss the United States, Russia, Japan, China, any nation that belongs to OPEC, Germany, France, and the United Kingdom.

4. RECOGNITION

This is important. Like having an older brother to protect you from bullies, it is equally important to have a strong relationship with another country that will back you in a political or military confrontation. In other words, you do not need to have a nuclear arsenal when you have a treaty with a nation that does have one.

Entering into a treaty or pact with another country that protects your nation or provides formal diplomatic recognition will have a price. Be prepared to offer to host an airbase or naval anchorage or to grant preferential arrangements for access to fisheries or mineral resources, or to grant exclusive marketing rights for key products.

In terms of economic health, you can guarantee a positive cash flow by enacting banking laws that are favorable to depositors from outside your borders, no matter what their motivations or source of funds might be.

If your new nation is blessed with attractive scenery, good beaches, and warm waters, big-game fishing, rare animal species, or other such attractions, promote the nation as a tourist destination. You will need an airport, which should be funded by another country and may also serve as the spot for hosting their air force presence should you grant basing rights. A major hotel or resort is good, though you may prefer to appeal to the well-heeled and socially/environmentally burdened souls of Westerners by presenting a more nature-friendly and bucolic cultural experience: ceiling fans instead of air conditioning, thatched roofs in place of tin sheets, and minimal availability to reliable sources of electricity. Be sure to produce at least one "native" beer.

5. NATIONAL ANTHEM

No country is complete without a national anthem (as well as a flag, seal, motto, bird, tree, etc.). You can write words and lyrics to your own if you are musically inclined, hire a professional to do it, or simply steal the melody from a popular song and change the words.

DRIVE A TANK THROUGH A TORNADO

What You Will Need

• One M1A1 Abrams tank—available from the U.S. Army, contact the Pentagon, to arrange purchase or lease.

• One flatbed tank carrier—also available from the army

• Mobile Doppler radar unit (or radio data link to the National Weather Service's Storm Prediction Center (SPC) in Norman, Oklahoma) with crew to monitor it and relay reports to you via radio—lease the radar unit from a meteorological department.

• Two-way radios

• Good maps

• One tornado

• Crash helmet

• Earplugs

⏰ Time Required

Varies, depending on weather conditions. Allow one week minimum, up to a maximum of six weeks.

☞ Background

Tornadoes are rated on the Fujita (F) scale, from the common F0 (40–72 miles per hour [mph]) to the theoretical F6 (319–379 mph). F0s and F1s (73–112 mph) make up about three-quarters of all tornadoes on record. The rating and wind speed of the tornado are essential items of information. It is best to focus on F0 and F1 tornadoes. Those at F2 and above can toss boxcars around, roll cars, and do considerable damage to structures.

An M1A1 Abrams is considerably heavier than a boxcar or passenger vehicle—weighing 60 tons carried low to the ground. This characteristic, which aids in protecting the tank from enemy fire, is also a protection against high winds. The armor plating, a variety known as Chobham, is very tough and will shield the vehicle's interior and occupants from anything that might be encountered in a tornado.

Not only is the Abrams hard to roll over, but it is also very fast given its size, capable of 30-plus mph over rough ground. On flat ground, it can go over 40 mph. Since it is not practical to predict the exact path of a tornado, this speed and agility will be essential to your success.

The primary reasons for targeting an F0 or F1 are the ease of finding them and the unknown potential for damage that the stronger tornadoes may cause the tank.

IMPORTANT NOTE

Do not let the sheer size of a tornado confuse you as to its strength. A larger tornado doesn't necessarily mean stronger winds, and a small twister isn't necessarily safer. To gauge tornado strength accurately, you must measure wind speed. Doppler radar will do this. If you have a mobile unit, use it to monitor each twister you consider before making an attempt. If not, download the specific tornado real-time statistics from the SPC before proceeding.

 Instructions

I. STAGING

Observe weather reports closely. Statistically, northern Texas and western Oklahoma are the best target areas. More twisters have been recorded in Texas than anywhere else in the world. The best time of year to find them is May through July, depending on location.

Stage yourself and your equipment south and west of

Norman, Oklahoma. Be ready to move out on short notice. The tornadoes, when they begin to form, will come from the southwest, moving northeast. Keep the Abrams on the flatbed, covered with a tarp and fully fueled. Make regular checks of its readiness to operate, including engine starts, within the manufacturer's recommendations. Be sure the tank's ammunition storage lockers do not contain any live or armed munitions.

2. MONITOR

Be patient and watch the weather reports constantly. The SPC will issue severe "storm watches" as storms begin to develop. A watch means severe weather is expected, but does not guarantee a tornado. If things begin to worsen, the SPC will issue storm warnings. If a tornado is sighted, a tornado warning will be issued.

3. MOBILIZE

Once you've determined the location and movement of a tornado-generating storm, proceed toward it as quickly as possible. Continue to monitor the weather information for further updates.

In a few cases, the SPC's watch will contain the words THIS IS A PARTICULARLY DANGEROUS SITUATION. This means that the SPC has determined that the storm will probably include a period of particularly strong, long-lived tornadoes. If you hear any such warning, focus all attention on this storm.

Deploy your mobile Doppler radar to track the storm and give you precise directions toward it.

4. TOUCHDOWN

As you near the storm area, keep watch for fully formed twisters or the characteristic cloud formation that indicates a funnel is forming: a cone-shaped section of clouds apparently being pulled down from the cloud layer. The radar will determine its direction of travel and speed and guide you in front of it.

IMPORTANT NOTE

Confirm the strength of the tornado at F1 or below before proceeding.

Stop the flatbed one to two miles ahead of the tornado, as close to its path of travel as possible. Start and off-load the tank from the truck and drive straight for the heart of the tornado. The flatbed should clear the area immediately.

Close and dog-down all tank hatches. Put on your helmet and take a seat in the driver's position, at the front center of the tank. Make sure the Abrams's turret is not locked down. Let it turn with the wind to prevent any damage to the machinery. The tank's main cannon, however, must be secured and unloaded.

Tornadoes may spin clockwise, but most often spin counterclockwise. Before you move into contact with the tornado, observe it to confirm its direction of spin. If clockwise, intercept the leading edge of the tornado from the left. If counterclockwise, intercept from the right. This will initially present the minimum surface area of the tank to the wind and ensure the tank will have maximum power to hold its ground and proceed through.

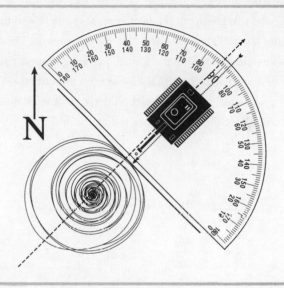

Approach the tornado from the northwest, with all hatches on the tank secured. Observe the direction of rotation. If the tornado is rotating counterclockwise, intercept its leading edge from the right. If clockwise, intercept from the left.

Continue forward, watching the tornado through the driver's view slit as you drive forward. Your view will be moderately limited, but adequate for your purposes.

The wind will buffet the tank, but you should be able to continue moving forward. Assuming the tornado was spinning counterclockwise, initially, you will feel the tank shifting to the right in the wind. Steer the tank in the opposite direction, using small movements. Don't oversteer.

Once the tank has passed through the center, the winds will hit you from the right, pushing you to the left. Again, steer gently into the wind with small adjustments to the tank's controls.

After about 30 seconds, you will exit the tornado. Drive directly forward, away from the funnel, watching around you for other twisters. Check in with the radar team to notify them that you are okay and to check the conditions. Arrange a meeting point away from the storm before exiting the tank.

BORROW THE *MONA LISA*

What You Will Need

- One bonded and licensed security firm
- Security officer uniforms
- Delivery company uniforms
- Two identical armored transport vehicles—these can be special-ordered from Ford or Daimler-Chrysler.
- A security team, including one driver and one guard for one truck
- A team to man the second truck
- Two similar automobiles with experienced stunt drivers
- A friend in the U.S. Department of State and a major U.S. museum
- High-quality wooden packing crates, labeled PRICE-LESS WORK OF ART—THIS END UP
- Two-way radios
- One abandoned industrial space
- One hideout

⏰ Time Required

One to two years for planning, setup, and establishing of credentials. Approximately 45 minutes for the removal of the painting.

☞ Background

The *Mona Lisa* has been stolen from the Louvre once, back in 1911. The theft was successful only in the sense that the thief got out of the building with the painting. Ultimately he was caught, and the painting was recovered. The main reason the authorities were able to recover the painting is also the primary reason that the thief was successful in taking it in the first place—stupidity. The Louvre didn't do a good job looking after the painting, and the thief was not suspicious enough when confronted with a cash offer to buy it—the offer was a sting.

It appears that law enforcement in France has gotten smarter. Now the *Mona Lisa* is well protected from sticky fingers through electronics, surveillance, and patrolling guards. While the 1911 theft was beautifully simple (which does have a certain appeal), it is not practical to repeat the technique used then (wait until no one is around, remove the painting, and get out through an exit stair). The security in the museum is now too good, which suggests that perhaps you shouldn't try to steal it in the first place.

Your best bet is to make arrangements to grab the painting

while it is not on its home turf—either while it is at another museum where the security is more easily compromised or while it is in transit. Both of these scenarios are high risk for the painting, which means high opportunity for you.

To prepare yourself for this experience, get some specialized training from the pros. The U.S. Department of the Interior (DOI) offers a three-day course in museum security. There is no charge, and, while the course focuses on the care of property in non-DOI museums, it is a good place to start in terms of understanding procedures and techniques.

The other essential element you will need is to persuade the Louvre to part with their priceless treasure. This means you will need friends.

 **Instructions**

I. ESTABLISH THE FIRM

You need to be the owner and operator of an (apparently) legitimate courier service. If you don't have a long and stellar history in the business, buy one. If that doesn't suit you, or the firms in question aren't available for sale, hire the key people in the industry. For enough money, you can bring the *crème de la crème* of the museum security industry onboard. This gives your organization an instant resume to use in the next step. (By the way, the best and brightest in this field are employed by the Federal Bureau of Investigation's Criminal Investigation Division [CID]. In particular, check for individuals employed in the

Violent Crimes and Major Offenders Section, Major Theft/Transportation Crimes Unit.)

In anticipation of "owning" the *Mona Lisa*, you'll need to acquire false papers quietly. This can be done through discreet enquiries in the less savory parts of London or Amsterdam. And it wouldn't hurt to significantly change your look before you go any further. Consider shaving your head, wearing a high-quality wig, growing facial hair, wearing tinted contacts, etc.

It would be a good idea to wear gloves any place that is connected to you or the acquisition of the painting to avoid leaving fingerprints. Wearing white cotton gloves while handling artwork is not at all uncommon, but you may have to put on an eccentric act to get away with wearing them at other times. If you affect to be a gifted madman, reliable in spite of having a few quirks, it may serve to endear you even more to the art world and allow you to get away with keeping your fingerprints to yourself. Alternately, you may wish to have your fingerprints "burned" off by a plastic surgeon.

2. GET THE CONTRACT

Your next step is to get the transportation contract from the Louvre. This will not be simple. You are going to have to compete for it. The Louvre has existing arrangements with bonded firms already, and they may not be immediately willing to give you a chance.

Given this, there is only one suitable approach to take— bribery, extortion, and smear tactics.

Swallow your ethics, put your morality on the back shelf,

and start to work to "persuade" the director of security at the Louvre that your firm is the only one to do the job. Since some people are immune to bribes, be prepared to go to blackmail immediately. In other words, if he doesn't bite on the cash, hire a private investigator to obtain compromising information to throw in front of him, along with an ability to recite chapter and verse the punishment for the misdeeds in question. Adulterers and embezzlers are good targets. Knowledge of past felonies or relationships with known criminals are also very persuasive arguments.

IMPORTANT NOTE

If your targets are too clean and have no documented nastiness blotting their records, create some.

In the meantime, set out to damage the reputations of your competition with mysterious accidents, fires, evidence of connections to organized crime, failures in securing other paintings, etc. All of these will serve your purpose.

3. ARRANGE THE LOAN, ARRANGE THE SWITCH

Once you have the transportation contract, you'll have to perform the first few jobs assigned to you perfectly to build trust and confidence. In this respect, hiring pros will pay huge dividends.

At this stage, your contacts in the State Department and a major American museum will begin the process of contacting the Louvre's directors and arranging a loan of the painting. This is a time-consuming process and may require payments of various sizes and patience. A request from a museum will not be adequate, but the weight of the State Department will tip the balance in your favor.

Your staff, especially those driving the dummy vehicle, will have a lot of explaining to do, especially since you'll have briefed them that this is a prearranged test of security and that the painting they are transporting is actually a copy. Once they understand that the real *Mona Lisa* is gone, they'll spill what they know. Keep them in the dark.

The prime time to make the switch is when the transport vehicle is momentarily lost from view, especially if there are chase vehicles or helicopters observing the route. A vehicle tunnel or a ferryboat is the best spot. You'll want to have a second vehicle (the dummy) that is a match for the one carrying the *Mona Lisa* ready and stashed in or near the place you're making the switch. The second vehicle should be disguised with removable panels or covers.

Before you get to the tunnel, contact the two stunt drivers in their vehicles and give them a heads up as to your estimated time of arrival at the location. They will enter the tunnel ahead of you and have an accident, temporarily blocking traffic. Their goal is to create a delay, but not to immobilize their vehicles. They must appear to exchange information and drive away on their own. If you decide to do the exchange on a ferry, there is no need to arrange an accident.

Once the vehicles are in the same place, strip off the covers from the dummy and put them on the real transport.

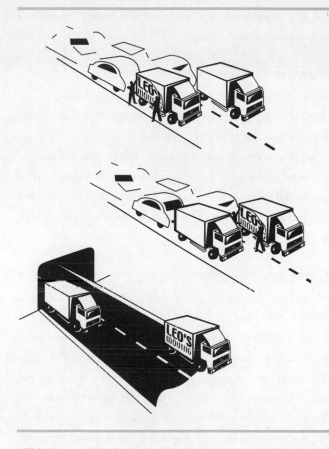

With the two vehicles in the same location, move the covers from the dummy vehicle to the real transport, then exit the area and take separate routes away from the site.

Upon exiting from the tunnel or ferry, have the security drivers proceed immediately to the delivery point in the dummy, while you drive the real transport carrying the painting to the secure location—the abandoned industrial space you scouted out in advance.

4. DISAPPEAR IN PLAIN SIGHT

The French authorities are going to close every border crossing, airport, shipping center, rail yard, etc., so plan on staying in Paris for at least the next three months.

Find yourself a place to stay, keep a low profile, and quietly return your appearance to its original look. It might help to wrap yourself in bandages for a while, at least in public, and tell people you are recovering from the side effects of a radical skin peel.

5. RETURN THE PAINTING?

Once you have the painting, you must deal with the question of what to do with it. It is one of the most beautiful and well-known works of art in the Western world. You may consider returning it in exchange for a reward, though this will increase your chances of getting caught. You could try to sell it, but that also increases the risk of being caught or blackmailed during the transaction. You could also return it anonymously with some recommendations regarding the museum's security policies.

Your final option is to keep it. If you decide to do so, maintain it in an environment with close control of lighting and humidity (to protect the painting), and with furniture selected to complement it.

Should you decide to keep the painting, install appropriate lighting and humidity controls, and select furniture to complement it.

WATER BOMB A FOREST FIRE

What You Will Need

- One Martin Mars flying boat
- 300 gallons of concentrated foam retardant
- One flight crew
- Ray-Ban aviator-style sunglasses
- One good-sized lake or ocean, suitable for landing and takeoff while at speed

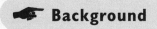 Time Required

Allow six hours per mission, plus prep and cleanup.

☞ Background

Water bombing forest fires is a particularly simple and effective way to deliver millions of gallons of water and fire retardant on a wildfire, especially when it's far away from roads or easy access.

There are all types of water bombers out there, most modified from commercial or military aircraft, and they range from a massive Russian transport to small one-seaters and helicopters. Which one works best depends on whom you ask and the conditions you're dealing with, but one of the most versatile and reliable is the Martin Mars flying boat.

Unlike other more familiar types of aircraft, the Mars (which were originally designed as long-range military aircraft) can drop a load of retardant on a fire, land on a conveniently located body of water and reload without ever stopping, and be back over the fire in a matter of minutes. Under optimum conditions, they can deliver a full load on the fire every 15 minutes.

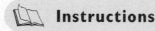 **Instructions**

I. FILL IT UP

Once you're called up for a fire, take off and head for your water source. Bring the Mars in just as you would for a normal water landing, allowing the speed to drop to about 70 miles per hour (mph) as the plane's belly cuts through the water. Pass throttle control to the flight engineer, and set scoop control to down. The twin intakes on either side of the keel line will pull in about 2,000 pounds of water every second, and the flight engineer will adjust the throttles up to maintain the plane at a skimming speed as the weight increases.

After about 25 to 30 seconds, the plane's belly is full, so

raise the scoops and call for take-off power from the flight engineer. Remember, you are now about 50,000 to 60,000 pounds heavier, so the plane is going to be more cumbersome to fly.

Once you're up and to speed, have the crew inject 30 gallons of foam retardant into the water tanks. The vibration of the plane will mix it up, but it will stay inert until drop. It's the tumbling action of the drop that will cause the mixture to convert to foam before it hits the fire.

2. VECTOR IN ON THE FIRE

As you approach the fire, check in with the fire commander. Airborne control will route you in to the target area. You may be allowed to make the run on your own, using your best judgment, or, if the conditions are rough enough, a spotter craft from the airborne control may lead you in.

If you're running in on your own, you'll want to aim for a perimeter area at the head of the fire, or hotspots (individual fires burning away from the primary fire, often threatening to start additional major fires).

Come into the target area from downwind. Be sure to report in when you are about three minutes up from the drop point. Begin to throttle back until your airspeed is about 140 mph, and set your altitude for the drop to about 200 feet. In rough terrain, particularly hilly or mountainous country, you may have to adjust your approach to allow to pull up and out.

Don't forget that throughout the approach into the fire, you need to be aware of where other planes are. You're required to maintain 500 feet of vertical separation from other aircraft. Also, though it probably won't be an issue in a remote area, watch for wires. They're the number one destroyer of aircraft, and it's easy to miss seeing them while you're bucking the up-draft and turbulence coming off the fire, not to mention the smoke and soot streaming up from the forest below.

3. DROP THE RETARDANT

Coming in on the drop zone, aim to drop about 200 to 300 feet from the target. The retardant will slow rapidly as it drops, though wind conditions will make a difference. Open the drop

At an altitude of 200 to 300 feet, approach the fire with a full load of water and retardant, aiming for a point 200 feet ahead of the fire.

doors and be ready—the plane will probably lift at least 100 feet as the water/foam dumps.

Close the drop doors when you've finished the run. Pull up and away, and report when you are clear of the drop zone so the next bomber can come in.

4. RELOAD AND REPEAT

Repeat the pickup procedure and head on back to the fire. Don't forget to check in, and aim for an area adjacent to the last drop. You want to make a partial overlap to ensure maximum value of the drop. Each drop, executed properly, will cover about four acres of ground.

With good conditions and a full load of foam retardant, you should be able to make 21 drops in about six hours.

Keep in mind, though, you're going to be working in close proximity to ground-based fire crews and smoke jumpers. Be ready to reroute to meet their needs, and do not dump the retardant on them. It won't harm them, but it will interfere with their operations and foul their equipment.

SHUT DOWN AN OUT-OF-CONTROL NUCLEAR REACTOR

What You Will Need

- One Pressurized Water Reactor (PWR)
- Construction plans for the reactor, including the electrical diagrams
- A pair of rubber gloves and insulated boots
- Protective eye-wear
- Hearing protection (ear-cuffs or earplugs)
- Hard hat
- Wire cutters

 Time Required

About 30 minutes.

☞ Background

Commercial nuclear reactors operate in a state of balance. In order to produce electricity, a core of nuclear material, enriched uranium in most cases, is allowed to get hot. Uranium emits neutrons which, when they strike other uranium atoms, cause more neutrons to be released, which in turn hit more uranium atoms. So on and so forth. If you have enough uranium emitting enough neutrons, the reaction can cascade out of control. (Do this very fast and under pressure and you get an atomic blast.) The trick in a reactor is to control the neutrons to make things hot, but not too hot.

The core's heat is passed to water surrounding the core. The water is kept under pressure so that it will get hot but not boil. This is why this type of nuclear reactor is called a PWR.

The hot water is circulated on a closed loop (the water is kept separate from other water, and is constantly recycled) inside the reactor containment vessel. It passes through a large container called a heat exchanger. The hot water from the reactor passes through this tank, radiating heat to the surrounding water, which turns to steam. The two water supplies never mix. The steam is fed into turbines, which turn generators and make electricity. From there, the steam returns to a cooling chamber where it condenses back to water before being recycled back to the heat exchanger to pick up more heat and be converted back to steam. Any waste heat from the process is either dumped into the atmosphere or a nearby body of water.

The balancing act of keeping the core at the right temperature is critical. If temperatures get too high, you "dampen" the reaction by inserting neutron-absorbing material into the core, usually in the form of a rod. This is the "control rod," and it collects neutrons that would otherwise cause the chain reaction to continue.

To take a reactor down in a less-than-scheduled manner is called a SCRAM. According to anecdotal evidence, SCRAM stands for "safety control rod ax man." The story behind this goes that during the first reactor tests by Enrico Fermi, the reactor's control rod was held out of the core by a rope. A man was stationed with an ax at this rope. In the event of an emergency or free-run condition in the core, the safety control rod ax man was to cut the rope and drop the rod into the core, shutting it down by absorbing neutrons and dampening and slowing the chain reaction.

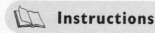 **Instructions**

I. MANUAL INSERTION

A critical condition at a nuclear reactor will be obvious to you. When the reactor gets in trouble, alarms will sound in the control room.

The simplest and most straightforward way to stop the problem is to insert the core's damping rods, which are composed largely of boron, into the core far enough to shut the reaction down. Boron absorbs neutrons very efficiently, making the reaction slow and stop. This should not be confused with cooling the core. It will take many hours for the residual heat to dissipate.

Use the reactor's manual system to lower the rods into the core, setting them in completely.

2. FLOOD THE CORE

To be safe, flood the reactor core with liquid dampener. Again, from the reactor control panels, initiate the release of the dampener. This liquid is little more than water laced with boron to a concentration of 2,000 parts per million. This will further stifle the reaction, and the reactor can be restarted later once the boron has been flushed out of the core.

3. DIRECT ACTION

Instructions 1 and 2 above assume you have easy access to the reactor control systems, and they are fully functional. If this is not the case you must follow a bare-knuckle approach.

One of the safeguards in a PWR is a modern version of the ax man. The control rods for a PWR are held in or out of the core by the constant supply of electricity to the motors supporting the rods. In the event of a major equipment or electrical failure, gravity will pull the rods all the way into the core. This is a standard feature on modern reactors and is known as a fail-safe mechanism. Fail-safe refers to the fact that in the event of a system failure, the particular component of a mechanism fails in a safe position as a standard in its design.

Shutting off the power, then, to the control rod motors is the final method and that of the last resort.

The rod motors are supplied with electrical power from

what is called a normal source. This is the standard power supply, usually fed from the commercial electrical utility grid. This source is backed up with emergency supplies, either from a diesel-fired generator, a battery source, or both.

Put on your hard hat, eye and ear protections, boots, and gloves before proceeding. Locate the normal and emergency power panels feeding the control rod motors. Open the panels, locate the circuit breakers for the rod motors and flip them to

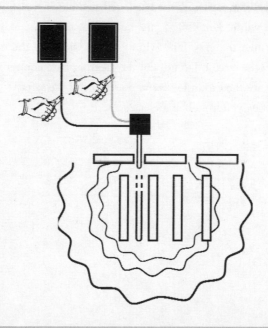

Once you have located the normal and emergency power panels and identified the voltage level, cut the colored wires as noted in the text. Cut the white or gray wire last. Do not cut the green or bare copper wire.

the off position. If they are locked, remove the panel covers and doors with an insulated screwdriver, noting the wires exiting from the circuit breakers (located to the left or right side).

Determine if the power circuits are 120 volt (v), 208 v, or 480 v. The power panel or the circuit schedule inside it will contain this information. Put on your insulated gloves. Cut the hot wires supplying the motors, starting with the normal power, then the emergency.

In the case of 120 v, cut the black wires first, then the white. For the 208 v, start with the black, red, and blue wires, followed by the white. For 480 v, cut the brown, orange, and yellow wires, then the gray. The white or gray wires are the neutral lines in the circuit. Do not cut the green or bare copper wires. These are the ground wires and are part of the safety systems protecting you from being electrocuted.

WIN A BULLFIGHT

What You Will Need

• One fighting bull about four years old, weighing between 1,200–2,000 pounds. The bull must have no prior experience fighting a man on foot. The term fighting refers to the type of bull, which is bred for its belligerence, and the attitude of the bull. Each bull is observed to judge its aggressiveness prior to the bullfight.

• One *traje de luces* (suit of lights)—the tight-fitting costume worn by the bullfighter, hand-tailored for you in Seville or Mexico City.

• One *muleta*—the small red cape used for the final part of the fight

 Time Required

Allow one hour for the fight, including preliminaries, presentation, entry to the *plaza del toros,* and post-victory activities.

☞ Background

The *corrida* (bullfight) is both a show and an exhibition of skill and daring. It tests man and animal (the bull and the horses used by *picadores*—horsemen who provoke the bull with lances) in a contest of speed, intelligence, and raw brutality. The *matador,* the star of the bullfighting world, is dressed beautifully in his *traje de luces* and almost dances around the bull, who, in turn, does his best to gore or kill the *matador* and anyone else in the way.

The bulls are bred for strength, speed, and aggressiveness, and the result of this centuries-old practice is a class of animals that stands a reasonable chance of success against the *matadors.* They are raised in conditions very close to those in the wild. Normally, these bulls range over thousands of acres set aside for them. They will only encounter a dismounted human once prior to the *corrida,* in order to test their speed, ability, and suitability for the fight.

The bullfight started in the Middle Ages when Spanish nobles fought bulls from horseback. Over time, the bullfighting of today came into being as a poor man's alternative. A horse was an expensive animal to maintain, and most people did not have access to one that they could risk losing in a bullfight. Because of this, *matadors* started fighting bulls on foot, and the sport has grown from that.

The nature of the *corrida,* whether a grand cultural tradition, a sport, or simply a show of brutality, is part of an ongoing debate, but it is worth noting that the bulls stand a better chance against the *matador* than they do against a meat-packing machine.

 Instructions

I. *PASEILLO*—ENTRY AND INTRODUCTIONS

Before you begin, you must allow time to have a *traje de luces* tailored. These are handmade to fit closely without restricting movement. A *matador* must be able to make quick and graceful moves, while looking splendid in the process. All the items described here can be purchased in Seville, Spain, or Mexico City, Mexico. (In a pinch, a fine tailor can probably provide an adequate substitute.) It will take six people about one month to complete your *traje de luces,* and cost up to 500,000 *pesetas* (about $3,000 or 3,100 Euros).

A *traje de luces* is typically made of satin and decorated in gold sequins and trim. Your assistants' suits will be trimmed in silver. As to color, this is largely your choice. Do not use yellow, which is considered unlucky.

Purchase a white shirt and narrow black tie, a sash to wear at your waist (the sash is usually red, green, or black), pink knee-length stockings, and black slippers—similar to those worn by ballerinas. Finally, you will need an *astrakhan,* the characteristic two-cornered black hat, and a pigtail. The pigtail will be worn clipped to the back of your head and denotes that you are a *matador.* Upon your retirement, the pigtail will be cut off.

Enter the *plaza del toros* as part of the parade of contestants and bailiffs. Salute the *corrida* president. He is the official in charge of the fight and will make decisions about both the process and the award of trophies.

Other *matadors* and their teams may fight before or after you. Exit the plaza until it is your turn. You will be notified by *corrida* staff when it is your time.

2. WARM UP AND ASSESS

A trumpet will sound to announce the beginning of your fight (and the start of each phase of the fight—there are three). Enter the ring with your team. The president will throw the bailiff the keys to the pen holding the bull and then wave a white cloth to signal that the fight may begin.

Capeadores (footmen) will warm up the bull using large gold and magenta capes (*capotes*). If the bull appears to be reluctant to fight, the *corrida* president may have it removed and replaced with a different one. He will signal this with a green cloth. While you wait, use this time to assess the animal's behavior and tendencies, whether it favors a particular horn in its charges or swings its horns at the end of a pass, as well as its agility, its speed, and, in particular, its strength. Watch for unpredictable behavior, which could increase your risk of injury or death.

3. WEAKEN THE BULL

Bulls are intelligent animals, significantly smarter than horses according to some. This is why, when the *picadores* enter the plaza, their horses are blindfolded (and padded). Otherwise, the horses would refuse to close with the bull, while the bull would have no such reluctance.

The job of the *picador* is to provoke the bull to attack him, plunging a lance into the bull's neck to weaken the muscles there. It is not intended to kill or degrade the bull's ability to fight so much as it is to make the bull lower and straighten his head if he has a tendency to hook to one side or the other. It is a poor *picador* that stabs too deeply or causes excessive bleeding, because this weakens the bull and makes the contest between you and him less fair.

Following the *picadores,* it is time to set the *banderillas,* short, barbed darts with colored ribbons attached, in the bull's neck. Like the lances of the *picadores,* the darts are intended to make the bull straighten his neck and lower his head. Setting the darts may be done by the *banderillo,* each one setting two of the darts, or you may choose to do it yourself. If you choose to set the *banderillas* yourself, approach the bull at an angle with one dart in each hand.

IMPORTANT NOTE

The way in which you make the approach to the bull and set the darts is an indicator of your courage and skill. If you approach from a narrow angle, the bull has a better chance of charging you. Also, the higher you lift your arm when setting the darts, the more time you give the bull to react.

If you are feeling exceptionally brave and nimble, do not approach the bull. Stand still and let the bull charge you, feint left or right to fool the animal, then sidestep in the opposite direction and set a dart as the bull passes. Setting a dart takes deft touch, plunging the dart's point down into the bull's skin, though not too deep, as this will cause more injury than necessary or desired. This is exceedingly risky.

A total of six darts should be set, usually three per side of the bull, and they should be set lightly so that they do not stand up straight from the animal. This indicates they have been set too deeply and reduces the quality of the contest from the crowd's point of view.

4. TERCIO DEL MUERTE

The final stage of a bullfight is called the *tercio del muerte*. At this time, signal all of your team, the *picadores* and *banderillos,* to leave the plaza. The last act is for you and the bull only.

Salute the president with your *astrakhan* and ask permission to perform. You may dedicate the bull to someone in the crowd if you wish.

Your goal now is to entice the bull to charge you. You will work with a *muleta* (a small red cape with a wooden dowel running across the top edge) and a sword. Contrary to popular myth, the bull does not charge a red cape (or anything red, for that matter; bulls are color-blind). The bull is angry and intent on defending its territory and charges at the *matador* or where it thinks the *matador* is. The large and small capes used in a *corrida* are intended to confuse the bull on this matter, and the skill with which the cape is moved is important. If, for example, during a charge the bull catches sight of your legs, he may veer toward you rather than plunging straight on.

Your movements and ability to command and control the bull are the primary ways in which you will be judged. Being able to make the bull charge and the way in which you move to avoid it are key. You must move like a dancer, almost posing, making all motions graceful. Use the minimum of legwork to avoid the bull's horns, demonstrating your skill with the *muleta* instead. Make the bull chase the cape, don't let him catch it. Sweep it away from him, up, over, or aside.

There are approximately 40 different passes you make with the cape, depending on the bull's location, which side it passes you on, your orientation, and, above all, your skill. The two most basic passes are the right-hand pass, in which you will use your sword to expand the *muleta* out perpendicular to the bull's line of travel, and the left-handed natural. The natural is perhaps the most dangerous of passes. You must bring the bull close to your body, turning slowly as the bull passes, forcing the animal to curve around you. Done in series with other moves, you will wind the animal back and forth past you. As an added touch, lift the *muleta* at the end of a series and see if you can make the animal flip his horns up at the end.

Throughout the passes, you must watch the bull closely. As the fight proceeds, the bull is going to get closer to you and also gain a better understanding of how the contest works. A smart bull will quickly discover any sloppiness on your part, which he will exploit (and kill you in the process).

The bull will begin to weaken with each pass. You will know this since it will become less aggressive and make slower and less frequent runs at you. At this point it is time for the kill. Exchange your fighting sword for the killing sword, which is sharp and designed to penetrate flesh, whereas the fighting sword is more of a tool for prodding the bull and sweeping your cape.

When the bull stops actively charging you, approach it from head on, aiming your sword for a spot high between the shoulder blades. The bull's front feet must be together, otherwise the sword will hit bone. The head must be down. Approach the bull while lowering and raising the *muleta* to hold the bull's attention. Just before delivering the killing blow, drop the cape to

Approach the bull, raising and lowering your *muleta* to hold its attention. At the final moment, lower the *muleta* and thrust the sword in between the bull's shoulder blades.

the ground. If you are slow or clumsy, the bull may shift his attention from the *muleta* to you, in which case you are in grave danger.

Done properly, the sword thrust will sever the bull's aorta, and it will die quickly. If the bull is still aggressive and charges you, aim for the same spot. This is called the *recibiendo* and is very dangerous.

5. CELEBRATION

If you have performed well and made the kill gracefully, quickly, and cleanly, the crowd in the plaza will express their appreciation. Make a lap of the ring. The audience will shower you with flowers, hats, cushions, and most anything handy. The louder the applause, the better. If the crowd is truly pleased they will wave white handkerchiefs. The president may, if he agrees with the audience, award you a trophy from the bull, typically one or both ears and the tail.

If the bull is exceptionally strong and has put up a good fight and you were unable to kill it, he will be spared and sent to a stud farm for the balance of his life. The crowd may appreciate your performance and that of the bull sufficiently to award a prize. It is not unheard of for the *matador* to be given the bull, in which case you can retire it to your own stud farm or one of your choice.

RESCUE MIAs FROM A POW CAMP

What You Will Need

• One prisoner-of-war (POW) camp with armed guards, fences, and searchlights

• One assault team (20–30 individuals), trained in insertions in hostile territory and equipped and armed as appropriate. (Much of the same equipment used in Conduct a SWAT-Team Hostage Rescue, p. 1, is applicable.)

• Two sniper teams of two persons each

• Three paramedics

• Two MH-53J IIIE Pave Low helicopters—each aircraft can transport up to 38 individuals. The actual number of MH-53s used depends on the size of the assault team and the number of prisoners extracted.

• Three Longbow Apache AH-64 gunships

• Helicopter crews (two pilots, two flight engineers, and two gunners per Pave Low, one pilot and one gunner per Apache)

• Real-time or near-real-time reconnaissance and intelligence information, including satellite and aerial photos and information collected from on-the-ground sources

• In-flight refueling tankers, depending on distance from friendly airspace to POW camp—if the round trip is in excess of 600 miles, plan on refueling.

⏰ Time Required

Allow 90 days to plan, train, and initiate. Allow no more than six hours for the mission, including aerial insertion, approach and entry to the camp, and extraction. Assume a maximum of 30 minutes in the camp.

☞ Background

According to various sources, there are several hundred Americans (army, navy, air force, and marines) who cannot be accounted for from various wars (MIAs). While the remains of many missing soldiers have been identified, there is evidence to suggest that there are still some Americans alive and in captivity, long after the end of the most recent conflicts.

The rescue of POWs is not a new event in military history.

Long ago, POWs were ransomed, though this was typically only the case for the nobility. Toward the end of the Second World War, Allied forces dispatched B-17 bombers to retrieve POWs from German camps near Ploesti, Romania, before the Russian Army arrived. During the Vietnam era, a raid to free Americans at Son Tay was unsuccessful, as the prisoners had been moved, and the last great rescue attempt, the failed 1980 foray into Iran to free American hostages from the U.S. embassy, ended in disaster and casualties for the forces involved, but no rescue.

Nonetheless, a well-planned, well-informed mission with the right resources and an experienced team is capable of entering foreign and even hostile territory and freeing prisoners, as long as it is supported properly and you are comfortable participating in what is essentially an act of war.

Alternatively, to avoid the rescue flaring into a major conflagration, it may be attempted and funded by private sources. Given the risks and the rewards, this is probably the best scenario.

 Instructions

I. PLANNING AND RECONNAISSANCE

Identify the target. As simple as those three words may be, it is a major undertaking to locate POWs who have been held for any length of time. They may have been assimilated into the local population, and it is safe to assume that they will not be dressed in distinctive uniforms.

Satellite and aerial imagery are good starting places. Russian spy satellite images are commercially available, but we recommend using American resources where they can be acquired. Use images with a resolution of one meter or less. Also make use of on-the-ground resources and networks to collect information, rumors, and other bits of data that help you refine your efforts.

Once you have established an accurate notion as to the location of the camp, use your local contacts to observe the area for specific evidence.

2. ACQUIRE RESOURCES

Once you have developed a clear understanding of the problem you are facing, begin assessing the people, material, and support you will require to complete the task.

A well-trained and well-armed team supported by aerial transport and assault capabilities is essential. You will move quickly and quietly into the POW camp area, but circumstances may require your exit to be less quiet, including engaging or suppressing enemy troops, antiaircraft, and even aircraft.

All material supplied by a friendly government, including Pave Low helicopters, gunships, and trained assault teams, must be stripped of national and unit markings and designations, identification numbers, personal effects (wallets, watches, correspondence, etc.). Given the size and scale of the international arms trade and the availability of trained soldiers willing to operate in a mercenary capacity, it should be easy to write off any question as to origination of weapons, aircraft, or soldiers.

All persons involved must do so on a voluntary basis. If possible, gather a team that has prior experience working together and has a grasp of the language used by the guards at the camp.

Once you have gathered your team, you must set them up to train and rehearse the rescue under conditions that resemble the real circumstances as closely as possible. This means using reconnaissance photos to mock up the camp and surrounding area and running the plan in full dress and real time. This will identify any fundamental flaws and allow corrections and adjustments to be made.

3. RAPID INSERTION

All troops and aircraft should be assembled at a "friendly" airfield outside the border of the target country, as close as is reasonably possible while allowing for a stealthy approach. Avoid paths that are too close to radar stations, military facilities, or large population centers. Uneven terrain and mountains are very useful for shielding your approach from visual or electronic monitoring.

Move your troops into the friendly country in small groups to avoid being detected. They should travel in civilian attire, using commercial air carriers, and should all arrive at the airfield several days ahead of the event, to allow them to acclimate and prepare. Housing and prep areas must be secure from observation.

Plan the assault for night, around the time of the new moon, when it is darkest. If weather cooperates, plan for cloudy conditions. Instruct your troops to assemble their material and check it and the function of their equipment early in the day. Once completed, have a good meal. Be sure to make a last check of current intelligence before leaving. Any changes in the camp or behavior of the guards might indicate they are aware of your intentions or foul up your planning.

In accordance with the timetable, the helicopters and gunship escort should lift off and proceed along the defined flight path, following the ground's contour. Maintain a height of 50 to 100 feet, depending on trees and other obstacles. Plot a course for the MH-53s to fly that is parallel to one another but slightly staggered, with the Apaches on point and flanking the transports.

The MH-53s are large and robust and, when equipped in the Pave Low configuration, remarkably well suited to low-profile work. The original MH-53s (familiarly known as Jolly Green Giants) earned their stripes in Vietnam, rescuing downed airmen. The updated versions are specifically designed for deep penetration into heavily defended airspace, using terrain-following radar, forward-looking infrared (FLIR) sensors, global positioning system (GPS), and other equipment. They are also fast (165 miles per hour [mph], armored, and well armed (use the configuration carrying three 7.62 millimeter [mm] mini-cannons). As for the Apaches, they have a highly successful record and are regarded as the premier attack helicopter in the world.

Approaching the insertion zone, slow the flight of the helicopters. Have the Apaches take up patrol positions around the area, using infrared and night-vision systems to identify threats.

Land the MH-53s, drop your assault teams, and then have the helicopters lift off. All five of the aircraft will move off to a holding position, waiting for your call for support and pickup.

The insertion point should be about one mile from the camp, depending on terrain and line of sight. A rainy night will cover the sound of the helicopters better, and a closer approach could be made. The teams will assemble and begin the approach to the camp in two separate groups, with scouts in advance to clear any obstacles.

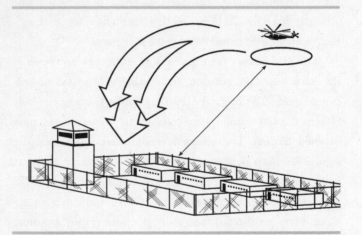

Land your assault team approximately one mile downwind from the camp. Your assault teams should approach in two separate groups with scouts in advance.

4. ELIMINATE OBSTRUCTIONS AND THREATS

You should already have a clear understanding of the camp's layout, the whereabouts of the prisoners, and your point of entry. Your initial approach is via stealth, cutting wires and accessing the camp as quietly as possible. Entering a facility of this type is not particularly difficult, since POW camps are typically designed to keep people in rather than the other way around.

One assault team will remove guards, subduing them as appropriate—lethal force is the last resort—and destroying any means of calling for help, including radios, computers, telephone lines (cut these), cellular phones, and portable radios or walkie-talkies.

Once the camp area is secure, proceed to the prisoner areas and begin securing the MIAs. Be sure to identify yourself to the

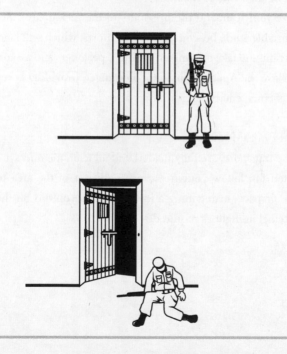

Disable all guards and release the prisoners.

prisoners as friendly and there to help. Make sure they understand you are taking them home, but exercise some caution. There is no way to account for their state of mind or stability. Many prisoners, after long confinements, begin to experience a state of empathy for their captors and may not initially be safe to leave unattended.

5. PROCEED TO THE LANDING ZONE

Call your transports to proceed to a pickup point in or adjacent to the camp. You cannot assume the prisoners are fit enough to move any significant distance over rough ground at night. You must bring their ride to them.

Move your team and the prisoners to the pickup area. Set out a portable guide beacon for the transports, which will land one at a time and take on a mixed group of prisoners and assault teams. Have the Apaches circle the perimeter, providing cover in case of emergencies.

6. ESCAPE AND EVADE

Once the transports are fully loaded and all team members are accounted for, follow your departure path out of the area to friendly airspace, maintaining a low profile as you did on the entry. Refuel in-flight as required.

CATCH A GREAT WHITE SHARK

What You Will Need

- One great white shark—South Africa, southern Australia, the Channel Islands, and the waters off the California seal colonies are the best places to locate one.
- One wet suit, mask, fins, and snorkel
- One large deep-water boat (40–50 feet) with large holding tank and motorized boom
- One shark sling
- One Zodiac inflatable boat with 100-horsepower outboard motor
- Tranquilizer and pole-mounted injection system
- Kevlar gloves—shark skin is rough.
- Several gallons of chum—a mix of animal or fish blood and entrails that attracts sharks.
- A large, fresh hunk of meat, the bloodier the better
- A boat hook
- Shark cage
- Duct tape
- Friends

⏰ Time Required

About two hours to attract and capture.

☞ Background

Great white sharks average 14 to 18 feet in length, and the largest one ever caught measured 21 feet (off Cuba). While great whites are not the largest members of the shark family, they are the largest predators, as well as the largest known man-eaters. (Whale shark are large, up to 50 feet, but are plankton eaters and pose no threat to humans.) With teeth like saw blades and the ability to move through the water at speeds in excess of 20 knots, great whites have a deservedly fierce reputation.

In terms of extreme thrills, then, it is not surprising that the popularity of swimming with sharks is on the rise. Most people do it with smaller sharks or from the safety of a shark cage if the shark encountered is on the large side.

IMPORTANT NOTE

Great whites are legally protected against hunting and exploitation by the state of California. Since you have no intention of killing the shark, you should be on legally defensible ground. It is questionable whether catching a shark is truly exploitation. The shark may not enjoy it, but the law says nothing about shark happiness. The government of South Africa also protects sharks against fishing, but not necessarily from being caught in a humane way and transported to an aquarium. Check local laws to be sure and obtain any necessary permits or licenses.

Winter is the best time for catching sharks. In California, that means November through March or so. If you go to South Africa or Australia, remember the winters there are the reverse of California's and plan on traveling in May through August.

 Instructions

I. ATTRACT THE SHARK

Have the crew on the big boat start throwing out chum to attract sharks. Be patient. It may take a while for them to arrive, but if they're in the area, they will show up. Launch the Zodiac and lower the shark cage into the water and secure it next to the boat with several lines.

When sharks begin to arrive, suit up in your gear and get into the shark cage with the tranquilizer. Keep the Zodiac nearby.

Have the crew fix the hunk of meat to a boat hook. Make sure it's secured well so you don't lose it. Try to attract one of the larger great whites to the boat by putting the meat-end of the hook in the water and waving it around to one side of the shark cage, pulling it back before the shark can take it. This is not unlike teasing a kitten with a string or toy, if you ignore the difference in bite radius. If you do this right, the shark will follow the meat right up along the boat's gunwale.

2. TRANQUILIZE THE SHARK

It has come to light in recent years that when a shark is in a vertical position, nose up, and you grasp its nose, it becomes

Once the shark broaches from the water, grab its nose. This will make it docile enough to tranquilize it.

docile. No one really understands the cause, but it has been seen consistently. (Interestingly, sharks also exhibit this behavior when they are rolled over onto their backs.)

As the shark broaches, a crew member must take hold of the tip of the shark's nose and hold on. At the same time, reach out of the shark cage and inject the tranquilizer into the shark's belly. Be quick.

Once the shark broaches, the meat should not be returned to the water.

3. WAIT

There's no way of predicting how the shark will respond to this experience. It might float in place, pondering what to do, or it might respond to the injection violently.

If the shark decides to really thrash about, abort the attempt. It is not worth injury to the shark or the crew.

If the shark remains docile, the boat crew should continue to hold the shark in place until the tranquilizer takes effect. While this happens, have the sling rigged and lowered over the side. As the shark begins to calm, the crew on the boat will gently rotate the shark so that it is parallel to the boat's side, but held in place. This is done by leaning over the side of the boat and grasping the pectoral and caudal fins and turning the shark. Wear gloves to avoid abrasions.

Get out of the shark cage and into the Zodiac.

4. SWIM AND SECURE

Bring the Zodiac up behind the shark. Once it is sufficiently quieted by the drugs, slip into the water and guide the sling to the shark, releasing one side of the sling so you can work it under the shark and pass it back up to the boat crew. It will take some jockeying, but you must position the sling so as to fully support the shark, with the help of the Zodiac and boat crew.

The boat crew will reattach the loose end of the sling to the boom and lift the shark into the holding tank. While this is happening, return to the Zodiac.

The shark should be kept damp, the water needs to be constantly fed with oxygen, and a current needs to be maintained past the shark's gills. Otherwise it will suffocate.

IMPORTANT NOTE

Throughout the experience, at least one member of the crew should be stationed with a boat hook to fend off other sharks and to serve as a watch over you. If he spots a shark headed your way, he must warn you immediately.

If another shark approaches, get out of the water immediately. If you are not quick about this, you may take some comfort in knowing about the historical record regarding great white attacks. In most cases, the shark does not actually eat the person. Most fatalities resulting from great white attacks are from blood loss. Scientists believe that the sharks take a first bite to taste their prey, rather than simply biting and swallowing. With humans, the majority of those attacked are released after the first bite. It is thought that sharks may confuse humans at the surface for seals, a favorite food, but, upon taking the first bite, they realize that the average human does not taste like seal, and discontinue the attack.

Nevertheless, even a minor bite by a great white can be serious. Having a good triage-rated doctor on board with suturing material and bandages is strongly recommended.

RETRIEVE MAYAN GOLD FROM A SACRIFICIAL WELL

What You Will Need

- Access to satellite and aerial photos
- Helicopter (Bell Huey or Jet Ranger recommended)
- Land Rovers
- Portable Global Positioning System (GPS) unit
- Inflatable raft with pump
- Technical diving gear with side-mount tanks, wet suit, mask, fins—depending on the depth of the *cenote,* you may need "stage tanks" for decompression—plus underwater lights, compressed air tanks, and tanks of other breathing gases (nitrogen, helium, and oxygen) for deep diving (if required), guide reels, and descent lines.
- Underwater writing tablet
- A dive buddy
- Portable magnetometer
- Rope ladders
- Derrick or large-lift bag

• Scuba "vacuum" system
• Camping equipment, including tents, sleeping bags, cooking equipment, portable generator, machetes, hand tools, and other items as required
• Archeologist(s)
• Work crew (approximately ten individuals with excavation experience)
• Permits from the local government—usually available at the provincial capital
• Insect repellent

⏰ Time Required

Allow two to three months.

☞ Background

The Mayan people built one of the most impressive civilizations in the Americas. Hundreds of cities dotted the landscape from what is now southern Mexico into Belize and Nicaragua. Some of the greatest cities are found on the Yucatán Peninsula (comprising the three Mexican provinces of Yucatán, Campeche, and Quintana Roo). This area is low-lying and swampy, yet there are no permanent rivers. Not on the surface, at least.

The area is a honeycomb of caves, *cenotes* (large sinkholes, often round, and sometimes referred to as sacred wells), and underground rivers, which resulted from a combination of the time when sea levels were lower and the composition of the underlying rock—limestone, which dissolves when exposed to naturally acidic water seeping into cracks in the ground. Over time, the water formed large caves and eventually the surface collapsed, creating the wells.

Because people and cities need water to survive, the Mayans in the Yucatán and Quintana Roo built their communities near the only freshwater they could access, in the caves and *cenotes.*

The exact extent of the Mayan civilization can only be estimated. For the most part, their cities fell and were abandoned between 800 and 925 A.D. The causes of the fall may have been famine, rebellion, or other as yet unidentified reasons. Whatever they were, by the middle of the tenth century, the majority of Mayan cities were dead. A kernel of Mayan culture survived in the Yucatán, intermingling with the Toltecs of central Mexico. However, by the time the Spaniards arrived, the Mayans had disappeared into the countryside.

Over time, the cities were submerged by the jungles and can be located only by accident or by people who know what to look for. When they are found and excavated, the ruins shed light on the Mayans' skills as builders and artisans, as well as on the depth of their beliefs. Tikal, one of the better-restored ruins, is studded with pyramidlike temples, many over 200 feet tall, and murals are still found, beautifully rendered samples of Mayan life and retellings of their mythology.

Mayan religious beliefs involved many of the same activities as other religions, including burying kings and great people with ritual objects and goods, bloodletting, and human sacrifice. There is also ample evidence that they offered worldly goods to their gods, often by casting them into the *cenotes* around their cities. Many of these objects were fashioned of gold.

 Instructions

I. LOCATE THE CITY

The first step to recovering Mayan gold from a *cenote* is to find a Mayan city with a *cenote*. There is little point in looking for gold in a previously discovered site, as other archeologists may already have searched the *cenote*. They are likely to object strenuously if you begin working their turf.

There are several ways to locate an as yet undiscovered city that is near a *cenote*. Visual inspection is a good way to start. The Yucatán is relatively flat, and the temples tend to stand out, even when covered by the jungle. Satellite and aerial photos are good ways of identifying clusters of "hills" that, when carefully examined, show a more geometric relationship to one another than would be expected to occur naturally.

Second, an examination of historical records and interviews with locals will provide clues and guidance to sites. The latter method may also supply you with a good guide, who will be essential to getting through the wild country to the city.

Finally, collect information from government and private

sources regarding the water systems in the Yucatán. A number of agencies and individuals have mapped the underground rivers. In particular, several nonprofit groups have worked in recent years to scuba dive these waterways, following them to or from the ocean, and they have developed excellent maps.

Look for regular groupings of hills or mounds in the jungle, particularly those near *cenotes* or sources of water. Focus your search in the Quintana Roo area of Mexico, south of the Yucatán.

When you combine and overlay the information you've collected, you will notice a few things that will help narrow your search. Focus your efforts on areas where water sources, particularly *cenotes,* are located in close proximity to "hills," which are most likely temples or other structures covered by the jungle. Historical records and interviews may also aid you here by providing stories or documents that tell of cities or ruins in these areas.

IMPORTANT NOTE

The sites in Yucatán province are well documented, and this is also the most heavily populated area. Focus your explorations in the northern portions of Quintana Roo province.

2. FIELD RECONNAISSANCE

Field reconnaissance should be conducted by air (helicopter), by vehicle (Land Rover), and on foot. As you identify potential city sites near underwater rivers or *cenotes,* examine them closely to confirm the extent and scale of the ruins. A larger city with a significant set of temples near a *cenote* is an excellent starting place.

A *cenote* worth checking will be near a temple site and will have signs indicating its importance, such as stone structures near it, steps down into it, or paving or stone platforms at the side nearest the temple(s).

Once you have found the well, drop sounding lines into it to determine its depth. This will determine the complexity of diving in it and the need for decompression stops and the applicability of technical diving guidelines.

3. PRELIMINARY DIVES

Return to the selected site with diving gear, underwater lights, the portable magnetometer, and rope ladder. You will also need ropes to lower equipment if the sides of the well are too steep or the water level too far below the edge.

Rig up your ladder, get into your wet suit, and descend to the water. Have the raft lowered and tied off. The rest of your gear should now be lowered by rope to you. Use the raft as a staging point to hold items while you complete your preparations. Put on your fins, mask, and diving rig. Make sure the air is on.

Your dive buddy should descend and prepare himself. Once your buddy is ready and has indicated such to you, signal you are okay to the support team at the top of the well and begin your descent.

Drop slowly to the bottom, turning on your lights as the water darkens and visibility decreases. Watch for trees or debris that may snag your lines.

Once on the bottom, proceed to the side of the well closest to the nearest temple. Any relics thrown in have a good chance of being in this area. Begin a surface examination of the *cenote* floor, following the wall of the well all the way around until you return to your starting point, then moving in toward the center five to eight feet and repeating the circuit, until you reach the center of the *cenote*. The goal in this dive (and depending on the size of the *cenote,* of follow-up dives) is to familiarize yourself with the layout and conditions. Watch for side passages and caves that may require exploration. Take notes on your underwater writing tablet of the features, bottom makeup (which is likely to be silt), and depths. These notes will serve to prepare a map of the site.

With the visual survey completed, begin revisiting the bottom with the magnetometer, noting the location of any hits. Again, complete the survey before proceeding to the next step.

4. EXCAVATION AND RECOVERY

Once you have located all magnetometer signals, prepare to ex-
cavate. Bring in the rest of your gear, including camping equipment, the generator, vacuum system, etc. Heavier items can be
brought in by helicopter. Otherwise, drive in as close as possible and pack material in.

IMPORTANT NOTE

Mosquitoes can be particularly vicious in the Yucatán
Peninsula when any standing water (such as a *cenote*) is
available for breeding. Given the newer, drug-resistant
strains of malaria, be sure to get a good antimalarial
medicine prescribed and use your insect repellent lib-
erally.

Any heavy objects such as relics made of gold or stone will have
sunk into the silt and muck covering the *cenote* bottom. Rig the
vacuum system at a secure location at the edge of the *cenote* or
on a float at the surface of the *cenote* if need be.

Focus on the areas that had the best hits on the magnetometer first, using the vacuum to suck in silt and deposit it out
of the well. All material excavated in this manner should be
screened and checked for small artifacts, bones, or other objects
of interest.

Larger relics will not be lifted into the vacuum, but will be uncovered as the silt is removed. As you identify them, take photos with an underwater camera and document the location of each item before removal. This will aid archeologists in understanding the site and the city.

After documentation, lighter relics should be placed in a basket and transported to the surface for further documentation. Larger items will require the use of the derrick or large lift bag.

5. REMOVAL?

Mexico, like most countries, frowns on the removal of artifacts from its archeological sites, and the United Nations has expressed serious disapproval of this practice. This has not yet persuaded the British Museum to return the Parthenon's marble friezes to the Greeks or the Louvre to return any of the statues they currently hold.

At this stage you have a choice to make. You can quietly spirit the relics to the coast where you may intercept a Panamanian freighter bound for Cayman or you can turn them over to the authorities. If you choose the first option, Quintana Roo is the best place to be. The local Indians and the federal government are in the middle of a dispute, and the *Federales* have little control in this province. (You may have to make a donation to the Indian cause.)

If you prefer to return the artifacts to the government, you should be sure you get the right permits BEFORE you start.

BREAK INTO
BUCKINGHAM PALACE

What You Will Need

- Taser stun gun
- High Altitude Low Opening (HALO) parachute training
- High Altitude Precision Parachute System (HAPPS) with primary and reserve chutes
- Aircraft and pilot
- Wrist-mounted altimeter
- Black Battle Dress Uniform (BDU) clothing
- Rucksack
- Servant's uniform
- Danner jump boots
- Oxygen mask, hose, and charged canister
- Altimeter
- Helmet
- Night-vision goggles
- Duct tape
- An English accent

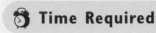 Time Required

One week for preparation and about two hours to complete the exercise.

☞ Background

Buckingham Palace is the official London residence of Queen Elizabeth II. She maintains many other homes around the United Kingdom, but Buckingham is the most visible, being in the heart of the city. As well as being Her home, the Palace also serves as the administrative headquarters of the monarchy. George III bought the building in 1761 to serve as a home near Saint James Palace, and it has been used on a more or less continuous basis by the Royals ever since.

A troop of household guards is in residence at all times (or, if operational duties take them elsewhere, another troop fills in), and the familiar red coats and bearskin hats are a sight few forget. They march with great precision and put on a great show of English pomp and circumstance; however, don't be fooled by their operatic costumes. These men and women are trained soldiers and heavily armed, and after regular hours, the sentries become (as the Brits say) "operational." One can take this to mean that, when the tourists leave, the guards are more prone to shoot to kill.

The Queen and Her family are not always in residence at the Palace. Before undertaking this project, be sure to check when Charles, the Prince of Wales, will be staying with His mother.

 Instructions

1. OBSERVE AND TRACK THE STAFF

Getting access into the Palace is not a particularly complex task. Once you are in, it is essential to avoid being noticed, and that is the real trick. It is, after all, just a large building in the middle of a big city.

The Palace has a number of servants and staff members, including those who serve and protect the royal family, maintain the grounds, and deal with visitors. Begin your foray into this project by observing the comings and goings of people from the employee entrance. Watch for individuals you are similar to in build. Once you have, follow them to their homes and ascertain their life situation. You need to locate someone who is single and works as part of the housekeeping staff.

Once you have picked the right person, approach them on a Sunday. Introduce yourself as a member of the American press doing a story on behind-the-scenes at the Palace. Employees of the Queen are polite people and odds are reasonably good that you will be invited in for a cup of tea. It is just as likely that your request will be turned down. This is not a problem, since all you want is to be in a quiet room with this person, out of sight.

Stun them with the Taser and restrain them with duct tape.

Locate their identity card. You will need it to move around in the Palace without being stopped.

2. STAND IN THE DOOR

Proceed to the airfield outside London where your aircraft is waiting. Your pilot will already have filed a flight plan that takes you past Buckingham Palace at about 30,000 feet, upwind from the Palace. Suit up in your HALO rig and be sure to confirm you've packed all your gear, except for the oxygen mask, and board the plane.

Suit up in your full HALO gear, remembering to connect your oxygen mask to your personal air source before exiting the airplane.

IMPORTANT NOTE

Be sure you checked and packed your own parachute.
Don't rely on others for this. Double-check all your gear
in flight.

As you approach the drop zone, put on your breathing gear and
complete the suiting-up process. Plug your oxygen mask into
the onboard supply until the pilot gives you a two-minute warning to jump.

Depressurize the cabin area and open the exterior door. It
will be loud, cold, and windy.

At two minutes to the drop zone, switch over to your own
oxygen supply and stand in the door of the plane. When sig-
naled, bail out.

3. JUMP AND WATCH YOUR ALTITUDE

You are going to drop from 30,000 to about 2,500 feet.
Watch your altimeter and check your location visually. London
has a very distinct appearance from the air, and you can adjust
your position by spreading your arms and legs to slow and "fly"
or pulling them in close to you to drop straighter. Adjust
according to where you are relative to the Palace and the wind
drift.

When your altimeter reads 2,500 feet, pull your ripcord. Be
prepared for the jerk. If the primary chute fails, use your reserve
chute.

Your parachute is not the traditional round variety used for many years, but is essentially a large wing. Once it is fully open, you can steer it and adjust your speed by tipping it left or right, or pitching the front edge up or down. Through a combination of these motions and with a little luck, you can make your approach directly onto the roof of the Palace.

Remember, as you land, to lift your feet slightly and roll the front edge of your chute up to slow your landing.

4. LAND ON THE ROOF AND ENTER THE PALACE

Once you have landed on the Palace, quickly collapse your chute to avoid any sudden wind gusts pulling you off the roof. Bundle the chute up and dispose of it along with all your other gear, putting the heavier items on top of the parachute to keep it from blowing away. Change into the servant's clothing, place their identification in an obvious spot, and find the nearest roof-access hatch.

Enter the upper levels of the Palace and locate the back stairs. Stay off the main stairs. Proceed to the residence level and locate a linen closet. Collect an appropriate selection of clean linens and associated materials, holding them in such a way as to partially obscure the identification. Avoid eye contact, but do not be obviously furtive or secretive. If greeted, be polite and personable.

5. THE PRINCE OF WALES SLEPT HERE

Once you have located the family wing of the palace, make your way to the bedroom of the Prince of Wales.

Short sheet the bed.

Move quickly to the staff exit and leave.

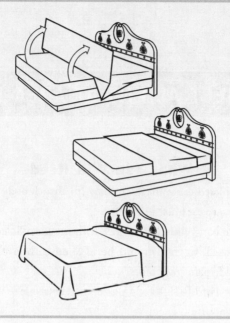

Once you have located Prince Charles's bedroom, carefully short-sheet the bed as shown, folding the lower half of the bottom sheet up to expose the mattress.

MEET ALIENS AT AREA 51

What You Will Need

- Insulated camouflage clothing (to absorb body heat)
- Kevlar vest (just in case)
- One hang glider, dark gray, with nonmetallic components—all rigging should be of spun carbon fiber, as should spars and frame.
- One Ford F-150 4 x 4 pickup and towrope
- Night-vision goggles
- Portable Global Positioning System (GPS) with landing coordinates programmed
- Radio scanner
- Climbing harness, descending rig, and rope
- Radio-controlled airplanes and cars (4-wheel drives)
- Tool kit (hacksaw, wire cutters, drill motor with regular and Phillips head screw bits, small bolt cutters, electrical and duct tape)
- Friends

⏱ Time Required

Allow one week.

☞ Background

Nellis Air Force Base is located in southern Nevada, west of the Nevada Range used for nuclear weapons tests by the U.S. government. The base was used as a site for testing advanced aircraft, such as the U2 and SR-71 spy planes and the F-117A

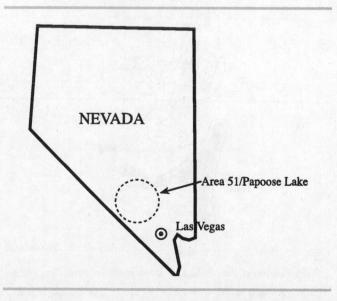

Area 51 is located in southern Nevada, near Las Vegas, at Nellis Air Force Base.

stealth fighter. This has only come to light recently, as the government has denied the base's purpose and existence.

There are many who say that the base has a darker secret, beyond stealth technology, that within the secret base is another

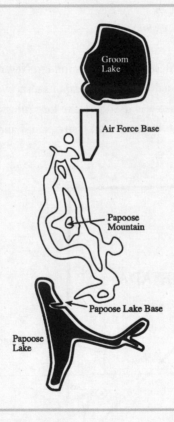

The real location of aliens in Area 51 is not at the well-known Groom Lake facility, but south on the western flank of Papoose Lake. A tongue of land extending into the dry lake bed marks the location to search.

facility, even more closely guarded. But what is being protected here, hidden from view?

Aliens, of course, and the flying saucers that the government has been studying since one crashed at Roswell, New Mexico, in 1947.

Some say the aliens are alive and well in Area 51 on the base, but there is evidence that suggests that they are actually located at a facility called Papoose Lake, south of Groom Lake.

Security at the Nellis Air Force Base and the Groom and Papoose Lake facility is excellent. An unfenced security perimeter has been established several miles out from the center of the facility, and it is extraordinarily effective. A fence simply isn't necessary. People approaching on foot and in vehicles are routinely intercepted, and even if they could get past the sensors and guards, they'd face the prospect of crossing some very rough desert. Warning signs clearly forbid trespassing and photography and warn that lethal shots may be fired.

The real issue is how are they detecting intrusions, and where are the weak spots in the systems.

The range of detection technologies includes older methods, such as passive infrared, microwave, and video motion detection, and extends into buried vibration sensors and electromagnetic field systems. These latter two are particularly nasty, because they can be buried and hidden from view and remain effective. These are supported by closed-circuit television cameras and radar that has had plenty of practice with stealth aircraft.

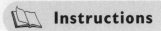 **Instructions**

I. PROBE FOR WEAK SPOTS

Before you begin to make your serious entry into the site, a little probing of the perimeter is in order. Use your radio-controlled (RC) aircraft and vehicles to cross into the restricted areas. Penetrations should be at various times of day, and the responses should be recorded. The reason for using the RC models is that they can cross the security boundary without any risk to you or your friends.

During all probes, be sure to monitor the radio frequencies, specifically around 141.55 and 142.5 megahertz (MHz). These are used by the security units. By tracking their traffic, you will have an idea how quickly and efficiently they are able to respond to an intrusion. If a lot of radio traffic comes up at the time you make your probe, you'll know they are watching and are more efficient. Less radio traffic means the perimeter is loose.

Keep track of the weather. You'll want to watch for good thermal activity, when rising heat from the desert floor will lift you, and when favorable winds will assist your ride to Papoose Lake.

2. CREATE DIVERSIONS ON THE PERIMETER

Once you have a sense of the thinnest parts of the security network, you will have determined your entry point. To distract security from you, have all but one of your friends approach the security perimeter on the opposite side of the base from your entry point. They should not congregate in one location, but at several different spots to spread the guards.

At no time should your associates cross into the security area. It is adequate to skirt the perimeter.

3. MOVE QUICKLY, MOVE QUIETLY

Until a few years ago, it was possible to get up on the mountains immediately adjacent to Area 51, but the government has annexed the surrounding land, adding most of the high ground (and thereby points that you could observe the base from) to their secured area. This precludes a launch of your glider from a hill or mountain.

Fortunately, with a good thermal updraft (this is why you watched the weather) and a stout towrope, the Ford F-150 can get you launched. After dark, and while your friends are providing cover for you, assemble the glider quickly and quietly and hook the towrope to it.

Your friends should signal you on the radio when they have succeeded in drawing the "dogs" off.

Strap into the harness and launch your glider by trailing it on a rope behind the Ford driven by your friend. Activate your night-vision goggles and keep an eye peeled for helicopters. If you see a helicopter and it appears to spot you, break off the attempt and turn toward safety.

Gain altitude as quickly as possible, and when you have reached the maximum height the towrope allows, cast it off and continue climbing. Once you have reached the maximum altitude possible, head into the Groom Lake airspace, and use the GPS to guide you to Papoose Lake. Keep a sharp eye out for helicopters and security patrols. In the event you believe you have been spotted, abort the run and head back for safe ground. Don't attempt to evade and continue the approach.

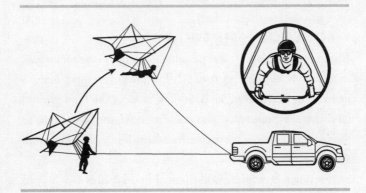

Use a Ford F-150 truck to pull your glider up to speed and get you to elevation. Be sure to wear a pair of night-vision goggles so you can spot security forces or helicopters.

4. LAND AND INFILTRATE THE BASE

Land near but not too near the Papoose facility. It is close to the tongue of the hill that extends out into the old lakebed. Once you are on the ground, check the immediate area with your night-vision goggles. Stash the glider out of sight and move quickly toward the entry to the facility. The site will have vents for its cooling and air-conditioning system, and these will produce hot spots as they vent waste heat to the atmosphere. This will be your entry point.

Find an exhaust duct at the surface. Check it for alarm systems or tamper switches, and bypass them as required. Remove the grille and secure your rope to the duct frame (remember to pad the rope where it crosses the metal frame to avoid cutting the rope).

Lower yourself into the duct system. Any screens or mesh in the system (put there to prevent people from doing exactly what you are doing) should be cut with wire cutters or hacksaw.

5. FOLLOW YOUR NOSE

Unfortunately, the exact location of the aliens is not known. The government does not casually publish or share this information, and the unofficial sources are unreliable and contradictory. However, there are a few basic facts in your favor.

• First, all evidence would indicate that the aliens are air-breathing.
• Second, they have been here a number of years, long enough to become acclimated to our atmosphere and the pathogens in it.
• Third, while the aliens are no longer in a closed area (in terms of ventilation), they are still alien. They reportedly give off a distinct smell, rather sulfurous in nature and distinct from humans.

Once you are in the heart of the duct system, locating the aliens is a matter of following your nose. Move quietly through the ducts, always toward strong smells that do not appear to be human in origin.

6. KLAATU BORADA NIKTO

Once you have located the vent into the alien quarters, carefully remove the exhaust grille and lower yourself into the room. Be sure to keep your hands visible and open so as not to startle them.

Given the length of time they have been here, it is reasonable to assume they have some command of the English language. Greet them.

RESCUE THE CREW OF A SINKING FISHING BOAT VIA HELICOPTER

What You Will Need

• One helicopter (Bell 407, Huey, Jet Ranger, or Blackhawk)

• One pilot, one paramedic who is also a rated rescue swimmer, and one rescue swimmer who is also trained as an emergency medical technician

• One long-line (100-foot length of 10,000-pound-rated ⅜-inch rope with attachment points at both ends)

• One seat harness

• One horse collar (a loop used for rescues)

• One-piece wet suit, 7 millimeters (mm) thick, with boots, gloves, and integrated hood

• Auto-inflate life vest

• One floating half-back (a floating device for stabilizing the back, neck, and head of the victims with possible spinal-column injuries)

- Floating strobe beacons
- Floating smoke markers
- Dye markers
- Glow-sticks
- Emergency medical equipment

Time Required

From the time the situation is called in to the time you get the victims to the hospital, about 60 minutes.

Background

There are several different approaches to helicopter rescues of people in the water. The right approach is dictated by the situation, the weather, and the equipment available to the rescue team. Different emergency service agencies use different methods, largely because their funding and their missions are different. The truth of the matter is that all the techniques are workable.

The U.S. Coast Guard, the organization most identified with helicopter rescue, tends to use larger aircraft with winches. Their process usually entails dropping one or more rescue swimmers into the water to load a victim into a litter, basket, or collar so they can be lifted into the aircraft. This process is repeated until everyone is out of the water, with the rescue swimmer going last (though on occasion, they come up with the last victim).

This method is very practical, though it is slower than some other methods due to the speed of the winch. The pilot's difficulties in maneuvering the helicopter during this type of rescue have been described as "parallel parking a large car while blindfolded, solely on the basis of instructions given to him by someone else." This is difficult flying by damn fine pilots.

Another method more often employed by local search-and-rescue groups operating over lakes or close to shore is the "long-line." It's fast and efficient and, for our purposes, the method of choice.

In this particular scenario, we assume the victims are two fishermen in a smallish boat off the Sonoma County coast of northern California. A bad fog has rolled in; the boat, without radar, has strayed too close to shore, getting caught in eight- to ten-foot waves. The boat has rolled over, the men are in the water in life vests but without survival suits. The waters here are frigid, around 60 degrees Fahrenheit, and hypothermia and drowning are serious risks.

 Instructions

I. THE INITIAL CALL

The first step in a long-line rescue operation is to take the call from the reporting agency. It may be from a local fisherman, the 911 service, or a passerby with a cell phone who notices a problem. Note all information—the location, the number of observed or known victims, their apparent condition, sea conditions, etc.—for the use of the rescue team.

2. GEAR UP AND WIND HER UP

As soon as the call is taken by the dispatch center, get your crew ready. The rescue swimmer (you) and the paramedic should get into wet suits while the pilot preps the helicopter, having the door on his side of the craft removed to improve his visibility. Also put on your seat harness at this time.

Once everything is prepped, load into the helicopter and take off, heading for the reported site to initiate a search pattern and begin rescue operations.

3. FLY THE SEARCH PATTERN

Unless you are very lucky or the report on the site of the accident is precise, the first step is locating the victims and ascertaining as well as possible their condition. Have the helicopter pilot proceed to the reported accident site and drop a dye marker or strobe into the water to note the current's direction and speed.

The pilot will then begin a circular search pattern, spiraling out from the center point while all three of you scan the sea for a sign of the victims. In rough weather or fog, a slow search is in order. If it is dark, use the helicopter's searchlights to assist, but keep an eye peeled for life jacket strobes. Don't hesitate to enlist the aid of other boats or aircraft in the area.

Circle until you have located the victims. Have the pilot hover to the side of them to avoid beating them up too much with the wash off the rotor, and try to assess their state—if they are responsive, if they appear to be injured, and how many of them there are.

Drop another smoke marker or strobe into the water to help you find the site, then return to the nearest point of land you can set down on.

4. DOPE ON A ROPE

Upon landing, rig up the long-line. Connect one end to the hook on the underside of the helicopter (in an emergency, the pilot can release it from the cockpit). Connect a locking cara-biner to your seat harness and to the attachment point on the end of the long-line. Because there are two victims in the water and one of them appears to be injured, you'll need to rig both yourself and the paramedic onto the long-line and take the half-back with you. You cannot have it lowered later.

5. INTO THE WATER

Once you are rigged in and ready, the pilot will slowly lift off until there is no slack on the line, picking you and the para-medic up. He'll return directly to the accident site, then lower the helicopter until you are in the water. Disconnect from the long-line and wave the pilot off. Because he has the door off the helicopter, he can see you directly. Instruct the helicopter to move a short distance away and hover to avoid hampering you with the rotor wash.

Connect yourself to the long-line, using a locking carabiner to clip your seat harness to the rope. Use hand gestures to direct the helicopter pilot.

IMPORTANT NOTE

There is no radio communication between the rescue swimmer and the pilot. The noise of the rotors and engine are so loud that audio communications are useless. All commands from the swimmer to the pilot are made with gestures:

• Arm pointing up and circling—go up.

• Arm straight out at side, waving slowly up and down—go down.

• Arm straight out and level—hold the helicopter level.

• Arm drawn toward you—return for pickup.

• Tap top of head with hand—change of plans, we're going to do this differently.

• Hands in front of swimmer—need a Stokes basket. This means returning to shore to rig one up. This is usually not a one-time crisis, as a Stokes is most commonly used only for the recovery of a dead body in this style of rescue.

• Arm out, folding over to touch top of head—I'm okay.

• Arms up and waving—I need help.

Once you're in the water, approach the victims carefully and calmly. Introduce yourself, tell them you're going to take care of them, and everything is okay, they'll be fine. It is essential that they do not panic, as they may endanger you or themselves further. A standard rule of rescue is never to make a single rescue into a double rescue by placing yourself at risk, so watch the victim carefully and keep him at arm's length if he appears to be panicking.

Do a quick assessment of the victims, making sure they are breathing and alert. Check for injuries, hypothermia, bleeding, or other problems.

Since one of the victims is in need of the half-back, both swimmers should get him into the harness. It takes two to do this usually; be sure to get the chest, shoulder, and leg straps connected snugly but not too tight.

6. HOOK THEM UP AND HAUL THEM IN

The victims will have to be removed from the water one at a time. Using the hand signals described above, gesture to the helicopter to return for retrieval and connect the half-back and the paramedic to the long-line. The pilot will lift off, leaving you with the other victim while the paramedic is transported to dry land, where he will begin any emergency medical treatment and stay with the patient, as well as rerigging the line for the second rescue. He'll rig a horse collar to the line, and the pilot will return to the scene.

The pilot will lower the line with horse collar to you, and you will slip the collar under the victim's arms and around his back. Reconnect to the line and attach your harness as well. Face the victim, hug him close with your legs wrapped around his chest or waist, and signal the pilot to take off.

He will lift you out of the water and return to where the paramedic is with the first victim. You'll be set down in the same area, and the helicopter can land. At this point, continue emergency medical treatment for both victims, get them into the helicopter, which is rigged to work as a flying ambulance, and transport them to the nearest hospital capable of taking a helicopter landing.

DEFUSE A HUMAN BOMB

What You Will Need

- Training at the Hazardous Device School at the Redstone Arsenal, Huntsville, Alabama
- Explosive Ordinance Disposal (EOD) suit, consisting of Aramid ballistic fiber covered with Nomex (fire retardant fabric). The suit includes a coat with sleeves, collar, and groin protector, trousers (covering the front of the leg only), helmet, polycarbonate face shield, and chest shield. A blower will also be included to pull fresh air in from behind you.
- Tele-operated EOD robot (optional)
- Portable real-time X-ray machine
- Bomb truck with total containment vessel
- Chemical sniffers
- Sandbags
- Explosives (including C4, dynamite, TNT, and Detcord)
- Miscellaneous tools and materials, including non-metallic cutting tools, picks (small tools for moving or separating wires, similar to a dental scraper), screw-

driver (flathead, Phillips, and Roberts head), mallet, insulating tape, and duct tape

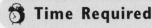 **Time Required**

About 60 minutes.

Background

EOD is the technical term for what most people know as the bomb squad. There are approximately 2,500 certified bomb-disposal experts in the United States, and they are a rare breed. Like special weapons and tactics (SWAT), they function in teams, but also frequently work alone to reduce potential casualties. The work is hazardous, more so since many bombers have begun shifting their attention away from targeting buildings and civilians to targeting the bomb squads themselves. The reasons are simple: taking out the bomb squad reduces the threat to the bomber and makes big headlines.

The ordinance and situations bomb squads must face range from mistaken identity (a harmless parcel left in an inappropriate spot) to sophisticated devices built with multiple detonating circuits and tamper-prevention components. While most devices can be defeated and destroyed, a few, those truly well conceived and built, can be nearly impossible to defuse safely.

The highest priority of a bomb squad is to save lives, but they also try to reduce damage to property. Thus members of a bomb squad place a high emphasis on defeating a bomb in place. A disrupter cannon (essentially a tripod-mounted 12-gauge shotgun) may be used to launch a slug of water or aluminum into a device, to tear its casing open or gut its circuits. Some explosives are banked up inside a bunker of sandbags built on the spot and detonated with a counter charge. If a robot is available (and functional), it may be used to destroy or remove the explosives.

Actually handling an explosive device is the least attractive choice despite advancements in protective gear. As one bomb squad member said, in the worst-case situation, the gear means you die leaving a good-looking corpse, though probably missing hands, which cannot be protected.

 **Instructions**

I. THE SITUATION

One of the most difficult scenarios for an EOD team is when a bomb is connected to a live person, either strapped to the chest of a criminal or, worse still, strapped to a hostage.

In the latter case, the first thing to do is to try to negotiate the surrender of the bomber or to send in the SWAT team to disable or take down the criminal. (See Conduct a SWAT-Team Hostage Rescue, p. 1.) If the bomb-maker was clever, he will have rigged a "dead man" switch—a detonator held in his hand that will explode the bomb if he releases it. In this case, the SWAT team cannot shoot him without endangering the life of the hostage. Negotiation will be attempted, and if it fails, the SWAT team will attempt to rush the perpetrator, overpowering him and taking control of the firing mechanism. They will use duct tape to hold the firing circuit open until the bomb can be defused.

Before the SWAT team moves in, establish a perimeter around the area, evacuating civilians and nonessential personnel. The basic guideline is if you can see the device (or where it is) from where you are, you are too close. A 300-yard clear area is advised.

While you wait for the SWAT team to disable the terrorist, put on your EOD suit. Ready your equipment and gear for a quick move into the bomb's area—speed is essential if the bomb is on a timer. Be prepared to move at a moment's notice.

2. APPROACH THE DEVICE

After the SWAT team has disabled the terrorist, they will clear everyone from the area, including the terrorist (in cuffs or in a bag). The only people left around the bomb will be the hostage and the SWAT member holding the triggering mechanism secure. Tape off the trigger with several wraps of duct tape to keep it from firing accidentally, then have the SWAT member leave. Disconnect the trigger if at all possible.

Once you have secured the firing device, approach the hostage (and the device) with your front toward them. If you move away from them, continue to face the bomb. The suit provides maximum protection to you in this manner.

IMPORTANT NOTE

Until you know the nature of the device, you may assume it could be triggered by radio. Avoid using anything but voice communications or cellular phones (which operate on separate frequencies than standard commercial radio transceivers) until you are sure.

3. PROVIDE PROTECTION TO THE HOSTAGE

The hostage is in a difficult situation. With some unknown quantity of explosives secured to his chest, he will be upset. In addition to disarming the bomb, you need to keep him calm. If he were to bolt suddenly, the jarring might be enough to cause a premature detonation.

Speak calmly to him, giving clear instructions, and telling him you are going to get him through this. Provide him with as much protection as you can. Have him lie down, and build a sandbag bunker around him. Equip him with a helmet, vest, face shield, and other items as required. This probably will not save him from the effects of a bomb going off on his chest, but it may calm him a bit.

Now for both the hardest and the bravest part.

Remove your protective equipment. This will expose you to serious consequences, but in this set of circumstances you need to be able to work as easily and effectively as possible. The EOD suits get hot and restrict movement. You will work faster and more effectively without it. Further, removing your suit will help persuade the hostage that you are not worried.

4. ASSESS THE DEVICE

Begin with a visual examination and assessment of the device. It may be an obvious bomb or it may be concealed or disguised. Pipe bombs and old ordinance (hand grenades, unused dynamite, etc.) are relatively easy to spot. Be careful, though. What it appears to be and what it is are not always the same.

Look for trip wires or booby traps. Listen to the device for

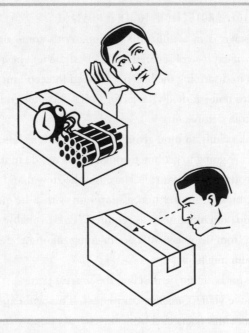

Beware of potential booby traps or timers in the bomb. Listen for ticking, and visually examine the bomb housing for trip wires or triggers before attempting to disarm it.

ticking sounds. Look for a timer, but be warned—an obvious timer may be a dummy or it may not be set to minutes or seconds. A bomber might rig a secondary timer as the real detonator, for example. Simple commercial clock timers are relatively straightforward, using mechanical action to detonate, and are thus not as difficult (assuming they are the real thing). For one of these, the mechanical contacts on the clock can be blocked with insulating tape. The long and the short of it is that you should not use a timer as a guide for how long you have to work.

You can use chemical sniffers to sample the area and identify the type of explosive. A visual inspection may reveal this as well. The type and quantity of explosive and the way it is packaged will help determine the probable effect of any explosion, and hence the risk.

If a visual inspection is not revealing, or you suspect a level of complication, bring in the portable X-ray and examine the interior of the bomb and the firing device.

5. DISARM THE FIRING CIRCUIT

If the firing circuits are not visible, get access to them carefully, watching for booby traps. Remove or unwrap any covers, remaining aware that a firing circuit may be incorporated into the outer covering. Cut if you must, but with great care, and use a nonmetallic blade. Ceramic blades are recommended.

Expose the firing mechanism and trace the wires to the bomb's battery. Determine how it is rigged. A simple loop circuit is easily defeated by disconnecting the battery or cutting the firing wires. Look for multiple firing circuits and power sources or a relay-actuated firing system. In the latter case, there are two circuits. The first has power applied to it to hold open a relay (essentially a switch). When the power to the relay is cut, it closes, and power is applied to a second circuit that fires the bomb.

You cannot deactivate a relay-type bomb by just cutting the power. If you cut the power to the relay, you detonate the bomb. BE ABSOLUTELY CERTAIN you have traced out the wires and determined which connect to batteries and firing circuits and which power the relay.

Since a clever bomb-maker will use a relay circuit, you must disconnect the firing circuit to the detonator first. The wire color is not important, since nothing compels the bomber to follow any standards or rules. Trace the wires that go from the relay to the detonator. (There will be at least two; cut both of them.) Once the detonator is disabled, the bomb is dead. RE-MEMBER: Some detonators, blasting caps in particular, can also go off if they become unstable or are jarred hard enough. Continue to exercise caution.

Remove the device from the hostage and have him escorted from the area. Remove the device from the premises by placing it in the total containment vessel (a reinforced tank designed to contain the blast) and transporting it to the firing range for disposal. If the device appears too unstable for safe transport, you may use a counter charge to detonate it in place (bank more sandbags around it to contain the blast first).

IMPORTANT NOTE

Forensic experts may wish to examine a bomb for fingerprints or other evidence. Be sure to keep track of all parts and material for later use.

DESTROY A NUCLEAR MISSILE SILO

What You Will Need

• One nuclear missile silo with LGM-30G Minuteman intercontinental ballistic missile (ICBM). You must have permission from the federal government to proceed.

• One missile transporter-erector vehicle

• One missile security team consisting of 15–17 armed Security Police (SPs) with backup of 4–8 additional SPs no more than 15 minutes away from the site.

• One missile maintenance team (four–eight missile specialists)

• Two-way radios

• Missile Electronic Encryption Device (MEEDs) units

• Nitroglycerine-based dynamite, about 1,000–2,000 pounds

• 18-grain detonating cord

• Electric detonators

• HBR-20P blasting machine

- Duct tape
- Concrete drills and drilling equipment
- Bureau of Alcohol, Tobacco, and Firearms (ATF) permit number 33, User of High Explosives, plus local state licenses or permits
- Heavy machinery, including earth-moving equipment
- General liability insurance covering property damage, combined single limit, explosion and collapse, for no less than $10 million

🕐 Time Required

Approximately eight weeks, including time for security checks, setup, removal of the missile, and demolition of the silo and support structures.

☞ Background

As a result of lessening tensions between Russia and the United States and several arms treaties, the need for a large force of nuclear weapons as a deterrent has been reduced, and both countries have begun the process of eliminating excess inventories of weapons, delivery systems (missiles, submarines, bombers, etc.), and support structures (such as missile silos). Over time, older weapons have been phased out (in some cases, the missile or aircraft has been reused for peaceful purposes, such as satellite launch, but often they are destroyed), and even some of the newer weapons have been eliminated.

The Minuteman III ICBM is one of the newer components of what has been termed the U.S. nuclear triad: submarine-based missiles such as Polaris and Trident, air-launched or dropped weapons such as gravity bombs and cruise missiles, and land-based ICBMs such as the Minuteman series and the MX Peacekeepers.

The Minuteman is one of the longest-serving weapons systems in the U.S. arsenal. The design of the series was first conceived in the 1950s, and the Minuteman I was deployed in the early 1960s, followed closely by the Minuteman II. Approximately 500 Minuteman IIIs were deployed in hardened silo structures in the upper Midwest and central United States around 1970. Each missile consists of a three-stage, solid-fueled rocket booster with a range of 6,000-plus miles at a speed of approximately 15,000 miles per hour. Each missile was originally designed to carry multiple independently targeted reentry vehicles (MIRVs), but under agreements between the superpowers, the warheads were limited to one per missile.

The silo structures for each Minuteman III are located in fairly empty country. Each one consists of a reinforced and hardened concrete cylinder about 50 feet across with a tube down the center for the missile. The silo is covered with a massive concrete and steel door mounted on tracks. The silo complex also includes electrical generation equipment, ventilation, command and communication systems, and connections via buried cables and UHF radio to the command center.

Early nuclear missiles were served by a dedicated missile combat crew in an adjoining structure. However, newer missiles are ganged together with ten silos under the command of a single crew (with backup launch control from other sources, including airborne crews in command aircraft). The crews monitor and maintain the missiles from a command center buried 100 feet below the surface and will serve as part of the team during the missile removal.

 Instructions

I. APPROACH WITH CAUTION

A nuclear weapon is always treated with the utmost respect and security by the soldiers who are assigned to guard it. Even a missile designated for removal and elimination is still capable of great harm in the wrong hands, and the warhead and the nuclear material (uranium and plutonium) in it are constantly guarded. Until the warhead physically leaves the silo area, plan for tight security with armed guards present at all times.

You cannot approach the missile silo without communications and security checks on a regular basis. Further, you will not be able to get to the missile to remove it without access codes, special keys, and the constant supervision of the SPs.

Begin by checking in at the main base. Your contact officer there will issue a set of codes to be used for verification throughout the work until the missile is removed as well as the keys required to open the silo doors. You will also be issued a

MEEDs unit, a small yellow box about the size of a handheld computer, which will issue and receive encrypted verification codes. Be sure your radio frequencies are properly set in coordination with the SPs.

Proceed in a convoy with the security and maintenance teams to the missile site, checking in every 15 minutes. (Remember, you will be working outdoors a considerable distance from any city or town, so plan ahead, bring all necessary materials, and dress appropriately.)

As you approach the fenced area around the silo, you will encounter layers of security-monitoring that protect and control the site, including buried sensors that detect movement before you get to the fence, sensors that detect any interference with the fence, and motion sensors that detect movement inside the fenced area. You cannot move to the silo through the security fence without the Missile Combat Crew (MCC) being alerted. Failing to communicate with them and the Flight Security Controller (FSC) will result in an armed response team being dispatched to the silo to investigate.

Contact the FSC by radio and verify your team's access codes through the MEED. The FSC will then contact the MCC and secure permission to enter the site. Permission will be given to you to proceed.

2. OPEN A, OPEN B, AND THE SILO DOORS

The security detail chief will contact the FSC and get access codes for the first of three doors that must be opened to access the silo. The A-pit is a small round steel access port which is unlocked using a combination and a key. This door will be opened by the security team. Once this is done, the security team will step aside and the maintenance team will access the next door, called the B-plug, which is a larger door much like the stopper in a bottle. The B-plug weighs about 14,000 pounds and is held in place by steel pins. Once unlocked, using another set of access codes, the plug will drop down and out of the way to grant access to the silo itself, a process that takes 30 to 45 minutes. The split of access between the A-pit and the B-plug is part of the security measures intended to prevent any individual from gaining access to the silo.

Once the B-plug has retracted, enter the silo and access the silo door controls inside the silo. Initiate the rollback of the silo door from the control panel to give you access to the missile. This will take another 15 minutes. In an actual launch or crisis, the silo door can "blow back" in seconds, but this is unnecessary for your work. Your work will also be under tight observation by Russian and Chinese military satellites, and a sudden silo opening will cause them alarm. Calm, cool, and by the numbers is the only way to work here.

3. DEACTIVATE AND REMOVE THE MISSILE

Before you can begin demolition work, remove the missile. Unlike earlier generations of missiles, the Minuteman III uses a solid-fuel booster, which means that the missile does not need to have its fuel supply drained off (a fairly dangerous task in and of itself). However, the missile is connected through hardened control lines to the MCC. As long as those lines are intact, there is always the potential for a launch. Your first task is to disconnect those lines, which can be accessed through the electronic umbilical that connects the silo and the missile.

Once you have opened the silo door and disconnected the umbilical, back the missile transporter-erector vehicle to the edge of the silo and raise the container on the back to an angle of 90 degrees. Done properly, the missile container will be pointing straight up and centered over the missile.

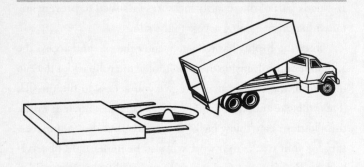

Once the silo door has been rolled out of the way, position the
missile extractor vehicle at the silo, directly above the missile.

Lower the missile extractor, a hydraulic system of cables, from the transporter and connect it to the adapter ring under the missile.

Once the extractor has been connected and double-checked, raise the missile slowly into the transporter-erector. Exercise great care not to let it sway or hit the sides of the silo. Speed is not important at this stage. Safety is.

IMPORTANT NOTE

In spite of the fact that the missile contains a nuclear warhead with many times the power of the Hiroshima bomb, it is now comparatively safe. The warhead cannot be detonated without proper authorization codes, and its firing circuits are hardened and will not respond to stray radio signals. The only risk is from fire, which could cause the high explosives surrounding the weapon's core to explode. The nature of these explosives is such that, unless they are fired in a particular timed sequence, the core will not go critical. However, the detonation of the high explosives will destroy the warhead and spread radioactive materials over the immediate area. There is also a risk of ignition of the rocket-booster fuel, but this is highly unlikely given the type of fuel.

Once the missile is fully within the transporter-erector vehicle, secure it for traveling. Lower the container, strap down the missile, and close the rear door. The missile and the security and maintenance teams will leave together in a convoy, heading to the main base, where the reentry vehicle and warhead will be removed. The missile will either be destroyed or reused as a launch vehicle for a satellite. The warhead will be decommissioned.

4. PREPARE THE STRUCTURE FOR DEMOLITION

With the missile removed and off site, begin preparing the silo for demolition. Disconnect and remove all reusable equipment. Drain the electrical generator's fuel tanks, and dispose of the oil per local and national environmental standards. The generator will need to be disassembled and hauled from the site for reuse or scrap, along with communications and control equipment. Power necessary for work lights or tools will be provided by local utility power or a portable generator as required.

Other items, including motors, lights, wiring, etc., can be removed and returned to the military or sent to a recycling/disposal facility as appropriate. The intent is to return the site to as close to its original condition as possible and leave no lingering traces or contaminants for the landowner to deal with.

Remove the fence and all security sensors, and disconnect or cut the control cabling. Have the electrical power lines disconnected by the local power company.

Once the excess material has been removed, dismount the silo door from its trackway and remove it via flatbed for recycling.

5. DRILLING AND PACKING

Demolishing a silo is not a complicated task, but it takes a fair amount of firepower. The structure is a cylinder approximately 80 feet deep, made of steel-reinforced high-strength concrete with walls in excess of ten feet thick. With earth packed around it, the silo was designed to survive conventional bombs and near-misses by nuclear weapons.

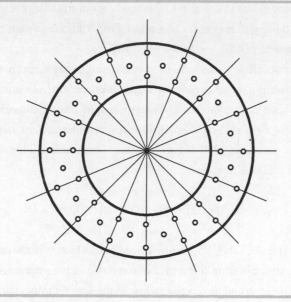

Drill holes into the concrete silo walls as shown. The holes need not extend all the way through the concrete. Pack the holes with explosives as appropriate for the volume of concrete to be demolished.

The best method of destroying a silo of this type is to implode it. This means shattering the concrete and dropping it into the silo. It is not necessary to implode the entire silo, just to shatter the concrete in the upper part of the silo and drop it into the lower silo, making it inoperable and irreparable.

Begin by drilling three concentric rings of 1½-inch diameter holes straight down about 40 feet through the concrete wall. The rings should be set in from the wall edges about two feet, equidistant between rings. The inner and outer ring of holes should be on a common line extending out from the center of the hole, with the center ring offset. Drill 16 holes in each ring, for a total of 48.

Pack these holes with dynamite, using approximately one-quarter pound of explosives for each cubic yard of concrete. The concrete volume can be determined by finding the volume of space defined by the depth of the cylinder and its radius, then subtracting the "empty" volume of the interior. This equation will look like this:

$$((\Pi * r_o{}^\wedge 2) * D) - ((\Pi * r_i{}^\wedge 2) * D) = V$$

Π is the value "Pi," approximately 3.14159, r_o is the radius (the distance from the center of the circle to its outer edge) of the outer cylinder, r_i is the radius of the inner empty cylinder, and D is the depth of the silo wall below the surface (all of these measurements are in feet). V is the final volume of concrete in cubic feet. Divide V by 27 to get cubic yards.

6. SHOOT! SHOOT! SHOOT!

Clear the silo area of all personnel and secure the area. A little paranoia is a good thing at this time. Arrive three hours early for the shoot and begin the final inspection of the initiation system. The safety and security crews should now begin to clear and cordon off the area.

About 45 minutes before the detonation, position spotters to observe the site, watch for trespassers, and make notes on the effects of the implosion.

At 15 minutes before the blast, the area should be clear, and security staff should leave the safety zone, an area extending out 200 yards minimum.

Communication is key at this time. Do a final communications check and be sure to keep clear channels open between involved parties.

At five minutes to go, hook up the blasting machine to the detonating cords.

With 120 seconds to go, sound the two-minute warning: two two-second sirens.

At one minute, sound a single, one-second siren.

With 25 seconds left, warm up the blasting machine and check it to make sure it is functioning properly.

At ten seconds to go, start counting out loud down from ten to six. At five, you count silently through to one, leaving the radio channels open so that security personnel can call STOP if they spot someone trying to enter the site. Once you reach one, call FIRE to all stations.

Depress the firing switch.

IMPORTANT NOTE

Many of the missile silos were established on private farmland rather than government reservations. In some cases, local farmers and landowners have lived with the missiles in their lives for 30 years, and quite a few of them are glad to see the weapons go. At your discretion, you may wish to offer the landowner the opportunity to depress the firing switch as a courtesy.

7. BACK-FILL AND COVER

Once the blast is over and the dust settles, move in with your heavy equipment to clean up any rubble and push the debris into the center of the silo. Excess dirt, concrete, and other material may be heaped into the hole and compacted to prevent settling.

RESCUE AN ASTRONAUT

What You Will Need

• One Soyuz model TM spacecraft, docked to the international space station (ISS) with navigational computer and remotely operable forward airlock

• Radar and laser rangefinder

• A good understanding of orbital mechanics and training in maneuver and rendezvous procedures

• A three–five man station crew

• A working knowledge of Russian, both spoken and written

 Time Required

Not more than six hours.

☞ Background

As part of the drive toward putting an American on the moon, NASA worked to develop methods of rendezvousing and docking separate spacecraft in orbit. The earliest attempts at docking, conducted as part of the Gemini program, showed just how difficult this could be. In 1965, Gemini 4 made a first attempt at rendezvousing with the spent second-stage of the launch vehicle. Pilot Jim McDivitt found that simply trying to move the Gemini capsule by instinct and visual observation was ineffective. It was nearly impossible to judge accurately the distance to the rocket booster without radar, and when he tried to move closer by aiming at the target and firing his stern thrusters, the distance between the two vehicles actually increased.

The reason for this phenomenon is found in the study of Newtonian mechanics, the mathematics of calculating and changing the movement of a body in space. When a body in orbit increases speed, as when you fire engines at the rear of the craft to catch up with another orbiting spacecraft, your spacecraft will increase its altitude. The speed of travel, also called the linear velocity, will increase, but because the distance from the earth is greater, the orbital path is larger and the speed with which the craft completes that orbit (measured as angular velocity) will decrease.

Gemini 4 had increased speed and thus had gone to a higher altitude. Even though it was going faster than the second-stage booster, it was trying to cover a larger orbital path and as a result slipped behind.

Since the time of Gemini 4, space rendezvous has become a regular event. American missions have met satellites such as the Hubble space telescope, and both American and Russian spacecraft have docked in orbit with each other, the MIR space station, and the new ISS so often as to make it appear easy. However, this is deceptive because there was ample time to plan and prepare, the orbit of the target was well known, and the launch of the spacecraft could be defined very precisely to minimize maneuvering. Most in-space meetings are carefully designed and executed to conserve the limited fuel supplies available. The safety of the crews depends on this.

At the same time, astronauts and cosmonauts have begun to work outside the ISS and their vehicles, in what commonly are called space walks (the space agencies refer to them as Extra-Vehicular Activities [EVAs]. When an astronaut leaves a spacecraft, he or she has become another separate body in orbit with all the risks associated, from exposure to impact from micrometeors or space junk and increased solar radiation levels. The risk of becoming separated from the ISS or spacecraft is addressed by tethers and the use of jetpacks, more properly called Extravehicular Mobility Units (EMUs) and Simplified Aid for Extravehicular Activity Rescue (SAFERs). EMUs are designed for free-floating, untethered movement (such as around the shuttle or Soyuz), whereas SAFERs are intended to be an emergency rescue device. Using these devices and safe practices, the danger of an EVA is reduced dramatically.

Still, there is risk.

Anyone who is launched into space must have the physical, intellectual, and psychological strength to deal with the stresses and risks that go hand in hand with the profession. The first cosmonauts and astronauts were military pilots, many with combat experience, and as such were not prone to panic.

The current nature of the space program is such that more and more specialists and nonmilitary personnel are going into space, and many do not have the specialized training that fighter pilots do. Furthermore, military or not, there is always a risk of a human being panicking in a dire situation.

Persons trained in rescue are consistently taught to control a situation and scene and to assign tasks and responsibilities to everyone. By demonstrating this degree of leadership, you inspire confidence, focus people on the important issue (the rescue as opposed to their fear or stress), and you avoid wasting precious minutes.

 Instructions

I. DON'T PANIC

Your first action is to take control and determine what has happened. In this case, a rupture of a gas tank has occurred while an astronaut was working on the exterior of the ISS. The astronaut's tether has been severed, and the explosion has swept the astronaut away from the station, pushing him down and away from you.

Immediately contact the astronaut. Is he conscious? Is his suit damaged or leaking air? What is the status of his primary life-support subsystem (PLSS), which includes the air supply and carbon dioxide scrubbers? This is typically good for about seven hours, though it will have reduced reserves if he has been outside for any length of time or has been working hard. Check the status of his secondary oxygen pack (SOP), which is good for an additional 30 minutes. Check to see if his SAFER unit is functional.

If it is, the first thing you should direct the astronaut to do is orient himself toward the ISS and use his SAFER to stop his drift and, if possible, return to the ISS. If he has insufficient propellant to make it back, at least this will diminish the distance and possibly stabilize his position relative to the station. If not, as in this case, the astronaut will take on an independent orbit moving away from the ISS and safety.

While you are assessing the situation, have the ISS crew monitor the astronaut's position using radar, noting speed and direction, and prep the ISS Soyuz rescue vehicle for operation. Fortunately, the Soyuz is kept in a hot-standby condition, making a quick launch possible. Have the crew work out an intercept path, based on the radar tracking information gathered, and load this to the navigational computer on Soyuz.

Contact ISS flight control, brief them on the situation, and advise them of your rescue plan. They may offer additional advice or support, but beyond that and good wishes, you're going to have to get by with the resources you have on hand.

2. LAUNCH THE SOYUZ

Enter the Soyuz. Bring one additional astronaut to assist with the rescue. Be sure you've programmed the astronaut's orbital statistics into your onboard computer. This will allow you to use computer guidance for the orbital maneuvers you'll need to make and greatly simplify the operation.

Close and seal the access port to the Soyuz and strap in to the pilot's seat. Decouple from the ISS and move away from the station using maneuvering thrusters until clear of any structural elements.

Using the navigation computer, align the Soyuz onto a parallel orbital path with the lost astronaut. Fire the forward

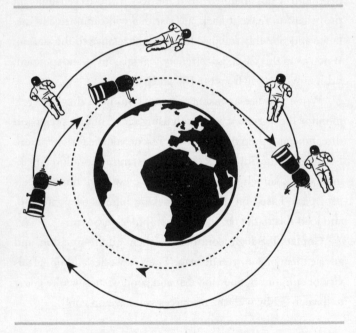

Slow the Soyuz capsule by firing the forward thrusters, causing the craft to drop to a lower, faster orbit parallel to the astronaut. Once you have caught up with the astronaut, fire your rear engines to lift your orbit to the same as the astronaut.

thrusters to brake the speed, causing the craft to drop to a lower orbit, below that of the astronaut. Your linear velocity will drop, but your angular velocity will increase, allowing you to catch up with your target.

Stay in radio contact with the astronaut at all times and make sure he stays calm and focused. Communicate your status to the ISS.

3. MATCH ORBITS

The navigational computer will signal when to apply thrust in order to raise and match your orbit once you have caught up. Approach from below and slightly to one side of the astronaut. The computer should be able to bring you within 50 to 100 feet of him. At this stage, go to manual control.

The Soyuz is equipped with several maneuvering thrusters that fire in the opposite direction of the vector the craft needs to travel. (Bear in mind, the craft can fly in an orbit but be oriented in any direction while traveling along that path.) The thrust can also push objects or astronauts away from you, so exercise caution as you make the final approach. You don't want to fire braking thrusters only to have the astronaut move away from you. A gentle touch on the controls, with small, controlled bursts from the thrusters, is much more effective and safer.

Approach the astronaut with the nose of the Soyuz pointing toward him. You will need to be close enough for him to grab the craft unless he has maintained a small reserve in his SAFER unit for this final move. Use your laser rangefinder to check the distance and monitor your closing speed.

The forward section of the Soyuz can be sectioned off between the outside vacuum and the control cabin with airtight doors. The forward door (the one opening into space) can be remotely operated from the control cabin. Be sure to vent the atmosphere from there before approaching the astronaut to avoid the outgassing pushing him away from you.

The forward section of the Soyuz can be used as an airlock.
Bring the nose of the craft close to the astronaut, but exercise care not to push him away from you when you fire forward thrusters to stop in his area.

Open the forward door and allow the astronaut to climb into the forward compartment. Once he is in, close and seal the forward airlock door. Your crewmate can then open the airlock into that compartment and go check on his condition.

While this is happening, program your craft's navigational computer for an ISS intercept and return to the station. Unless there is a medical emergency with the astronaut that cannot be addressed on the space station, there is no need for an emergency return to earth.

RESCUE AN INJURED MOUNTAIN CLIMBER IN ANTARCTICA

What You Will Need

• One rescue team (three–five individuals) experienced in high-altitude, extreme-weather work, with one emergency medical technician familiar with the treatment of altitude-related illness—a fully qualified doctor is preferred if available. The members of the team need to be in very good shape, able to cover rough terrain at altitude rapidly.

• Technical climbing equipment suitable for ice, snow, and rock work, including sleeping bag, sleeping pad, tent, double climbing boots with cold-weather liner, overboots, crampons, heavy pants and jacket, windproof overpants and overjacket, gloves/mittens, hat, balaclava with face guard, extra socks, long underwear, pack, rope, seat harness, ice ax, carabiners, prusiks,

sunglasses and goggles (UV-proof), multipurpose knife, sunscreen, lip protection, and zinc oxide
• One Twin Otter aircraft with skis for landing, with pilot
• Emergency food rations (high-energy foods suitable for eating without preparation and suitable for altitude)
• Water
• Portable two-way radios
• Emergency medical supplies (bandages, splints, antibiotics, painkillers, etc.)
• Portable hyperbaric chamber—a reinforced fabric bag that can hold the disabled climber while air pressure is built up in it using a foot pump. The better models include a pressure gauge and a window to allow you to observe the patient. Buy this from a mountain-climbing supply store.
• Portable oxygen tanks and oxygen mask(s)
• Acetazolamide (known by the trade name Dimox), a carbonic anhydrase inhibitor drug that can provide temporary relief for the deleterious symptoms experienced at altitude.

 Time Required

Allow 48 to 72 hours.

☞ Background

The Vinson Massif is the tallest peak on the Antarctic continent, cresting at 16,067 feet. It is one of the Seven Summits—the tallest peaks on the seven continents (the others are Mount Everest in Asia, Aconcagua in South America, Denali in North America, Kilimanjaro in Africa, Mount Elbrus in Europe, and Mount Kosciusko in Australia, though some claim that Indonesia's Mount Carstensz is the seventh rather than Kosciusko).

Vinson is unique not because of its elevation—it is only the sixth highest of the Seven Summits—but because of its remoteness and the difficulty in getting there. The peak is located at 78 degrees 35 minutes south latitude, 85 degrees 25 minutes west longitude, in the Ellsworth Mountains, 1,200 miles from the northernmost tip of Antarctica and only 600 miles from the South Pole. In the summer climbing season (November through January in the Southern Hemisphere), temperatures average minus 20 degrees Fahrenheit, and it often gets colder. Fortunately, it is perpetually light during the summer.

Access to Vinson is a multiphase process. Under normal circumstances, heavy-transport aircraft (usually military-grade planes, such as a Hercules C-130, that are capable of handling the harsh conditions, particularly bad crosswinds) are used to get onto the continent from Punta Arenas in Chile. The first stop on the way to Vinson is in an area known as the Patriot Hills, a private camp with a runway built into the permanent ice capable of handling the large aircraft. From there, access to the

Vinson Massif base camp at the base of the Branscomb Glacier is by light plane, usually a Twin Otter.

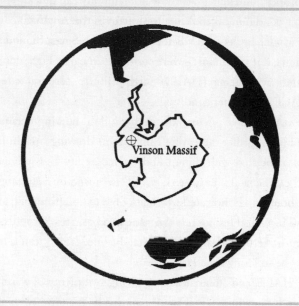

Travel to the Vinson Massif via Hercules transport from Punta Arenas to Patriot Hills base camp. From there, fly west to the Vinson base camp in a light plant, such as a Twin Otter.

The Vinson base camp is located at 7,000 feet, and the trip to the summit is a hike and climb of over 12 miles across the glacier and up a head wall.

As altitude increases, air pressure decreases. At sea level, air pressure is 14.7 pounds per square inch (PSI). At 16,000 feet, air pressure is about half that. Lower pressure means a lower percentage of oxygen in the air, which translates to increased difficulty breathing, especially when the body is working hard. Add to this factors such as fatigue, cold, dehydration, and lack of proper nourishment, and the human body can quickly spiral into a condition called Acute Mountain Sickness (AMS).

Milder forms of AMS include headache, nausea, and insomnia, but in its most severe form, it can cause high-altitude pulmonary edema (HAPE), high-altitude cerebral edema (HACE), and other conditions.

HAPE is like pneumonia, in that a fluid buildup occurs in the lungs, further increasing difficulty in drawing breath. It is also associated with diminished mental acuity and judgment and can be fatal if untreated. HACE is caused by a swelling of the brain and is indicated by a loss of mentation (thinking) ability. The easiest test for it is the same as a basic test for intoxication: make the person walk a straight line. If they can't, they may be suffering from HACE.

HAPE tends to arise slowly, giving you plenty of warning, though sometimes it may be discounted by the unwary climber as a cold or flu. HACE, by contrast, can arise suddenly and with little warning. Unlike HAPE, HACE is unmistakable and much more dangerous, likely to lead to death if untreated.

IMPORTANT NOTE

When asking someone to undergo a test for HACE, make sure they are walking unencumbered by their pack and are on level ground (if possible), and take the same test yourself to be sure any difficulty is related to physical ailment and not the test area.

Whether the climber has HAPE or HACE, the only cure is to get them off the mountain and to a lower altitude. If they are unable to walk, you must get them fit to walk out, which means medical treatment on site, enough to get them moving. If you can't do this, they're going to die.

 Instructions

I. SEARCH AND LOCATE

When the word comes down from the summit that a problem has been encountered, the first course of action is to gather your rescue team and assemble emergency gear and necessary supplies at the Branscomb Glacier base camp. As it may be necessary to fly the injured climbers out for more involved medical attention, make sure the Twin Otter and pilot are available and ready at this camp with the necessary fuel to make it to Patriot Camp.

You have a hard trek ahead of you to get to the climber, who is suffering a worsening case of HAPE. Time is essential, especially if the climber is incapacitated to the degree that he cannot safely descend. If this is the case, instruct the summit team to begin basic life support and first aid: rehydrate the patient if possible, keep him warm and dry, and monitor his symptoms.

The summit team is without oxygen or Dimox, so you'll need to bring it, along with your portable hyperbaric chamber.

From the base camp, the normal route to the summit is a roundabout path, east to the face of the glacier, then skirting up a head wall, and then to the peak. One-way, it's a two-day trip with fairly gentle gains in elevation. In an emergency, a team that is tough enough can push straight to the summit up the glacier in 14 to 16 hours, cutting the distance in half.

2. MEDICAL ASSESSMENT AND PRELIMINARY TREATMENT

Once you have reached the climbing team, you must assess the condition of the patient. It is essential to stabilize him as much as possible and get him on his feet. One of the unfortunate truths about mountain climbing in remote areas is that the conditions are so harsh that it is unlikely an injured or ill climber will be carried out. As one climber said, "Climbing is optional, getting down is mandatory."

The summit team has already done what they can, keeping the patient stable, warm, and hydrated. Begin administering oxygen and Dimox to the patient under the direction of the doctor (if present—if not, contact the expedition doctor at Patriot Hills via radio, either directly or relayed by the crew at the runway).

Dimox is a temporary measure. Its positive effect on AMS patients is thought to relate to the increased excretion by the kidneys of bicarbonate. This causes a condition known as metabolic acidosis, which increases respiration and thus oxygen, which will alleviate some of the patient's infirmity.

The administration of oxygen will also improve the patient's condition. This in combination with the Dimox may be enough to get them on their feet and headed down the mountain. It is the "down" part that is most essential now. A lower elevation is ultimately the only cure for HAPE.

3. REPRESSURIZE AND STABILIZE

Since the patient is too weak and ill to descend to a higher-pressure environment, you bring the higher pressure to the patient. This is the reason you packed the recompression chamber with you. Properly operated, your portable hyperbaric chamber will maintain a pressure equal to about 7,000 to 8,000 feet, more than enough to reduce the effects of the thin air.

Unpack your hyperbaric chamber and lay it out on a slanted surface so that the climber's head will be moderately elevated. Place the climber in the chamber in a sleeping bag to maintain body temperature. An insulating pad under him will also help keep him warm. Continue to administer oxygen to the patient in the bag.

Close and zip the seals and begin inflating and pressurizing the chamber. The pressure source for the chamber is a simple foot-operated pump. You'll need to run it more-or-less continuously to keep the pressure up, particularly if the chamber does not have a built-in carbon dioxide scrubber. Without the scrubber, the CO_2 will build up and asphyxiate the patient.

Pump up the chamber slowly to avoid tympanic membrane barotraumas (pain, damage, and rupture of the eardrum) and hold the patient at pressure for approximately one hour. Slowly release the pressure and check the patient's condition. Repeat this process if required for a total of two to four hours. At the

Put the injured climber into the portable hyperbaric chamber in a sleeping bag.
His head should be raised above his feet. Close and seal the chamber and begin
pressurizing it with the pump.

end of this treatment and in coordination with the oxygen and
Dimox, the patient will probably recover enough to hike down
to a lower altitude on his own.

4. WALK TO THE LANDING STRIP

Gather up the team, relieving the patient of as much of his gear
as possible (other than cold-weather gear and essential climbing equipment). Instead of taking the direct path out (as you

did in), follow the longer but easier route. By the time you get down a couple of thousand feet, you should see a marked improvement, which will only continue as you descend. Allow 24 hours to make the trip to the base camp and the plane.

5. FLY TO THE NEAREST MEDICAL FACILITY

Pack the team and gear (though be prepared to leave equipment if you don't have enough room on the Otter for everyone and their gear) and return to Patriot Hills. The camp has a doctor onsite during the climbing season, and he can handle basic emergency medical care. If a more serious condition is encountered, evacuate the patient to the better-equipped facilities in Punta Arenas. This is unlikely—if you've managed to get the patient down under his own power, he is probably going to recover fully, though he may be groggy and disoriented for a few days.

RESOURCES

A final word

The research for this book was conducted using a number of different resources. The library system, bookstores, magazines, periodicals, and the Internet were all great in many respects, though the exploration was painful and slow at times.

For many of the details, I was able to draw upon personal experience (though to date I have not borrowed the *Mona Lisa* or taken any gold from Fort Knox). I also made a number of telephone calls to places like the Pentagon. A careful request to the right people and interviews were set up, documents faxed, and answers given where possible.

The best source for a book like this, though, turned out to be my circle of friends (and their friends, too). Just within my immediate circle I found people with expert knowledge of explosives, hostage rescue, fire fighting, security, flying, controlled demolition, extreme sports, the best routes on the Vinson Massif, and animal and human physiology.

The lesson here is that for all the things you don't know, you might be shocked to learn what your friends do know. All you have to do is ask.

RESOURCES

If you'd like to share your own ideas with me (and perhaps prompt a sequel to this volume), I'd be delighted to hear from you.

Send your correspondence to:

Hunter S. Fulghum
c/o becker&mayer!
11010 Northup Way
Bellevue, WA 98004

ABOUT THE AUTHOR

In real life, Hunter S. Fulghum is a technology
therapist for a large international construction
company. When not soothing troubled minds over
the uncomfortable issues of computers and networks, he spends his time clambering up rock
walls or blowing bubbles 70 feet below the surface
of the ocean.